In Pursuit of Shadows

A Career in Counterintelligence

In Pursuit of Shadows

A Career in Counterintelligence

T M Slawson

ATHENA PRESS
LONDON

IN PURSUIT OF SHADOWS
A Career in Counterintelligence
Copyright © T M Slawson 2006

ISBN 1 84401 695 1

First Published 2006 by
ATHENA PRESS
Queen's House, 2 Holly Road
Twickenham TW1 4EG
United Kingdom

Printed for Athena Press

This book is dedicated to Brewer N. Newton, Lieutenant Colonel, United States Air Force (Retired) who demonstrated leadership by example and professionalism by practice

THOMAS M. SLAWSON is a practicing attorney in Florida. He served for twenty years as a counterintelligence agent in the US Air Force. During his career, he participated in every aspect of counterintelligence operations. He holds graduate degrees in Business Administration and Forensic Science from George Washington University as well as a Juris Doctor degree from the Catholic University of America. In recent years, he has served as a security consultant to an international energy corporation. He has studied and researched worldwide terrorism as well as the history of intelligence. He lives in Melbourne, Florida with his wife Nancy.

Contents

THE MAKING OF AN AGENT

I have enjoyed a career as a Special Agent, United States
Air Force Office of Special Investigations (AFOSI) and
during that career, I engaged in the practice of counterintelligence (CI). I started out in the United States Air
Force (USAF) with the intention of becoming a pilot;
several months into that training, the Air Force decided
that I would not.

The decision was made by a civilian flight instructor,
who bragged about the number of officer students that
he had washed out. It all happened very suddenly. We
were at 10,000 feet, and in his own cheery way, he
bellowed out, "OK college boy, give me a three-turn spin
to the left." I responded immediately. The nose of the
aircraft ascended to a nearly perpendicular attitude, and
as it did so, I pulled back on the control stick, kicked the
left rudder pedal and sent the aircraft into a beautiful
spin. It turned and dived toward the earth with ever
increasing speed.

I realized that the speed was due to the fact that I had
failed to reduce the power, which was part of the recov-
ery procedure. I reduced power immediately and slowly
pulled the aircraft out of the power dive into which I had
placed it. As the aircraft leveled off, I read fifty feet on the
altimeter. We were a bit low as I recovered and leveled
the aircraft. This close call was not the only thing that
caused my instructor to go ballistic. It seems that the
good man had a habit of undoing his seat-belt and
placing his clipboard on the instrument panel in front of

him; thus positioned, he gave me the lowest grade possible.

It appeared, from his anger and apoplectic condition, that he had been somewhat tossed about, as I made my absolutely last three-turn spin to the left.

Shortly after that experience, I flew a check mission in which a military instructor put me through my paces and then gave me a rating. Of course, it was "Below Average." He said, "Son, you can fly this airplane; but you are several hours behind your class and the Air Force won't give you any more time to catch up. We are 'over' on pilots and will only keep the best students in the program." During the flight, I accomplished all of the maneuvers without a word from the check pilot. I knew that the outcome was preordained even before I was told. I had given it my best shot.

In no time, my name was sent to Air Force Personnel for reassignment. Not realizing the proper procedures to be followed, I went to the local Air Force Office of Special Investigations (OSI) detachment to enquire about joining. I was encouraged by the local OSI Commander to fill out an application, which he would forward directly to OSI Headquarters in Washington, DC. He seemed pleased that I had a degree in accounting and said that the outfit could use officers with accounting degrees. He described, very generally, the duties of an OSI agent. The fact that agents always wear civilian clothes appealed to me. It was then that I was told about the CI role of the OSI, and I knew almost immediately that that was what I wanted to do. It took a relatively short time before OSI notified Personnel that they wanted me. I was given orders to report to Special Agent School in Washington, DC.

My orders stated that I had been assigned, as a student, to the OSI School which was located in Temporary "E" Building at Fourth and Adams Drive, SW in downtown Washington, DC. It is the place where the Air and Space Museum is now located. Erected during World War I, it was supposed to be temporary in nature. In 1957 it was still standing and serving the needs of the US Government. It was one of the few bargains that the US Government ever received. It was, however, on its last legs. The old, rusty window air conditioners were unable to lessen the Washington heat and humidity. They made noises that indicated that they were accomplishing something. Actually, they accomplished very little. The interior of Tempo E, as it was called, was painted a light green throughout. That color was widely noticed in federal jails and US post offices. There was no visible security either in or outside the building.

I reported to the OSI School, which occupied a small part of the building. There were about sixteen people in my class, all officers, ranging in rank from Second Lieutenant to Colonel. We were all in uniform and it did not appear that we would suddenly don civilian clothes anytime soon. Someone, in civilian clothes, was quick to tell us that he was ex-FBI and that he was an instructor in the school. He related how the OSI had been set up by Joseph Carroll as a centrally directed USAF-wide investigative agency that served under the Inspector General of the USAF. Carroll came on active duty as a full colonel and was soon promoted to Brigadier General. He was followed by FBI agents who were brought in as civilian agents. I was to learn that OSI was essentially a carbon copy of the FBI. All of the training materials were patterned after the FBI bulletins. Each dealt with a specific subject that was to be covered in the basic agent course. Like all FBI publications at the time, they bore a monotonous blue cover.

We were assigned a safe drawer to protect our classified materials. I was impressed as I read the titles of a few of the bulletins. There were *Surveillance*, *Crime Scene Search*, *Casting and Molding*, *Report Writing*, and *Fingerprinting*. There was a vast array of subjects that would be covered in the Basic Agent Course, but I saw nothing that dealt with CI.

We were told that it was an honor to be selected by OSI and that we had very high standards to maintain. Honesty and integrity were primary attributes of the OSI agent, and any failure to meet these standards would result in immediate dismissal. I knew that they were not kidding. There were a number of enlisted agents in the OSI with whom we would work and ultimately supervise. There did not appear to be any enlisted agents at the school. I would find out later that one of the instructors, who was particularly "officer-like," was in fact a Master Sergeant with many years of experience.

Throughout the fourteen week course we were constantly evaluated. Many of the other students were pilots who had not agreed to serve beyond their regular four year tour, or pilots for whom the Air Force had no flying positions. Many of them were neither interested in, nor happy with their assignment. They had spent the major part of their careers in flying assignments and were happy to remain there. Many of them would serve one tour in OSI and then retire, or if young enough, return to flying assignments.

Despite their lack of enthusiasm, most of the officers performed well in the school. The few, who had applied for OSI were enthusiastic and very competitive. They were good students, like me, who worked hard to excel. Criminal investigation was emphasized in the course and little emphasis was placed on subjects unrelated to it. This of course, was where the FBI supposedly excelled.

We all had to qualify with the .38 cal. pistol, which was at that time carried by FBI agents. The gun, which had a three inch barrel, was carried on the right hip, and seemed a most unsuitable weapon for concealment. The instructors were laughed at most heartily when they said that this monster handgun could be concealed. It was accurate and relatively easy to fire, but its size and weight made it a most unsuitable weapon for concealed use. Later OSI would acquire the "snub-nosed" .38 that, although concealable, was only accurate within a limited range. Some said that the FBI agents were recognizable by their wearing of hats (which they still did at the time) and the large bulge protruding from their right hip. Everyone was able to master the .38 to the satisfaction of the school, and carry it as unobtrusively as possible. We were not taught the use of any other weapon.

Another subject taught at the school was *Photography*. We were expected to learn how to use the 4 x 5" Graflex camera, which was used by reporters. For some reason, the removable film pack and the complicated nature of its operation made that camera difficult for most of us to use. If you could ever use it right, the camera gave sharp pictures with large 4 x 5" negatives. I was pleased when I occasionally got excellent "crime scene" photographs. I had difficulty in figuring out how a camera of that size could be used to take surreptitious photographs, as might be required in CI. It would be great for photographing crime scenes and other non-surreptitious types of photography. While the 35 mm camera was emerging as a popular photographic tool, OSI had not discovered it yet; nor was there any mention of telephoto photography. All the emphasis was placed on photographing crime scenes.

Once again, the use of photography in CI was not mentioned. Additional training was given in the use of the fingerprint camera. We used what looked like a homemade, wooden camera, which was placed on the print and one lever moved to take a picture of the fingerprint. The illumination for the photograph consisted of flashlight bulbs, which were illuminated when the single lever was tripped. It got extremely poor results. Someone explained that it had been acquired from the US Army Counterintelligence Corps (CIC), which was the Army organization that engaged in CI. That was the only time the CIC was referred to throughout the course.

Near the end of the course, we were told that we would study a block of instruction related to CI; I could not believe that only thirteen hours were devoted to that subject. Short "bulletins" devoted to *Espionage*, *Sabotage* and *Subversion* were issued. We did receive a recommended reading list of books found in the OSI library. I had discovered the library long before we began our CI block. I avidly read all the books about intelligence and CI, which I thought would supplement the training given at the school. I didn't realize that my extensive readings would far surpass any instruction provided by the school. We were told that the Soviets gave their agents months of schooling in intelligence and related subjects.

I was convinced that there was more to come and that

there would certainly be more time devoted to CI than the schedule indicated. I was told by one of the ex-FBI agent instructors that the time devoted to CI was considered adequate. Even though I was lacking in training and experience, I sensed that this was wrong.

According to the instructors, training in investigative techniques, though oriented toward criminal investigations, provided much of the training needed for CI work. This was the FBI attitude and it was adopted totally by the OSI.

My disappointment was somewhat lessened when we got to instruction in surveillance. The training was extremely thorough. Though oriented towards criminal investigations, it did mention the value of successful surveillance in CI work. There was a lot of practical work in both surveillance and countersurveillance work. We learned how to spot a "tail" and how to shake a "tail," the word for a surveillant. The instruction included "dead drops;" that is, placing documents in a hiding place for someone else to retrieve. Selection of the "drops" was taught thoroughly and the techniques for letting your contact know that the drop was loaded or that the contact should not approach the drop. This was all done with no direct contact.

Great thought went into selecting the place for a dead drop. It had to be accessible to the contact, not discernible as a hiding place, and difficult for the "opposition" to detect when it was "loaded" and "unloaded." One trainee struck out using a men's room in a prominent hotel. It appeared to have all the requirements, but, as the instructor pointed out, "Suppose the contact was a woman." I had selected the chapel adjacent to the Georgetown Law School. It met all of the requirements and was open late. A red chalk mark on a nearby telephone pole let the contact know that the drop was loaded and a white mark told the contact to avoid using the drop. We were taught to survey our agent who was wandering around Washington, DC, merrily loading our dead drops. We did this by having him (there were no women agents in those days) walk past a certain spot, where agents could observe who was behind him. He would then walk past another selected spot and agents would try to determine whether or not anyone behind him had been spotted at the first location. This technique worked well, if the countersurveillance agents were attentive and had good memories. One of the instructors followed our "agent" without being detected by the countersurveillance. He wore a hat and glasses, and deceived us, even though all the trainees knew him. He pointed out to us that a slight change in appearance will confuse those looking for a survellant.

Our joy at having devised good dead drops was diminished when we were told to survey a person identified to us. We were told the time and place to pick up this person and how long to survey him. Both men and women "rabbits" were used, and they were either people we had seen only occasionally, or not at all. A good physical description of each person was given, so that we would not waste the evening following someone not involved in the exercise. We all felt that we were really doing a good job, until the people involved were asked, after observing the class, to identify anyone they thought had been observing them that day. Almost all of us were identified as having been seen following one or more of the rabbits. One thing we learned for certain was the fact that a good surveillance must involve as many surveillants as possible, the more the better, to lessen the chance of detection by the person being observed. The FBI favored the "ABC" method. This involved the use of three surveillants, two following behind the rabbit and one behind and across the street. The two behind the rabbit could exchange places in order not to cause suspicion and the third, across the street and behind, would be able to assume the surveillance if the first two were identified or, for some other reason, left the surveillance.

There are many variations on a theme in surveillance work. The more people available, the more flexibility and increased security can be attained. I later heard that in 1962, when investigating Judith Coplan, a State Department employee spying for the Soviets, the FBI employed over eighty agents. Later, I would discover that usually only one or two people were available for a surveillance and it would be necessary to determine if the risk of discovery was worth the results to be achieved. The FBI has used aircraft in surveillances, for example, in the John Walker spy case in 1985, a technique not likely to compromise the operation.

The surveillance can produce significant information, aside from knowing where the person goes and who he meets. By demonstrating countersurveillance techniques, the subject can reveal that he has been trained and is using methods to evade surveillance. His awareness of such information indicates that he is possibly involved in surreptitious activities; alternatively, if he does not show knowledge of a surveillance he might still be involved in surreptitious activities and feigning a lack of knowledge about his being followed, as an innocent person might do. If the surveillants do not mind letting the subject know he is being followed, they can maintain close, continuing coverage of a person's activities. During the Cold War, the Soviets often let the subject know that he was under surveillance, and it became a game of cat and mouse with the subject evading and the Soviets picking up the surveillance again. This was designed to prevent US Intelligence agents from contacting their sources of information because of the fear that they were always under surveillance. I felt that surveillance and counter-surveillance were of the greatest importance in CI investigations. My later experience would confirm this.

The block of instruction, *Interviews and Interrogations* was, to me, the most interesting and the most professionally presented. Although obviously oriented to criminal investigations, the applicability of the techniques taught applied to CI investigations. First, it was pointed out that there is a distinct difference between an interview and an interrogation.

Clearly, an interview is asking questions of and receiving information from someone who, usually willingly, offers information, is not a suspect, and whose veracity does not immediately come into question. Witnesses to an event, who have no personal interest in it, and people given as references by someone are usually interviewed in a friendly manner. Of course, the questions must be specifically designed to get the required information and efforts must be made to keep the person on the right subject. Some rambling by the interviewee may be allowed if time is not of the essence and it contributes to rapport with the person. Questions should not be leading, e.g. "John Smith went to Central High School didn't he?" The "interrogation" is similar to the "interview" only by virtue of the fact that the person is also being asked questions. The similarity ends there. The purpose of the interrogation is to elicit information that the person does not want to reveal, information which may cause him to be arrested, or dismissed from his position. In a CI investigation, it may be the fact that he has been spying for a foreign country, or knows someone who has. The seriousness of the offense will result in anyone being reluctant to disclose facts that prove such an allegation. Like the criminal interrogation, the CI interrogation will be an attempt to get someone to disclose something that they strongly do not wish to disclose. First, thorough preparation must precede any attempt to engage the person in conversation. Questions like, "What do we know about this matter?" "What is the basis for our suspecting the individual of being involved in an offense?" "What facts link the person to an offense or to someone known to be involved?" And very important, "How much do we want to let the suspect know what we know?" In cases of less experienced persons, sometimes a show of knowledge will convince them to disclose what is desired. A trained person will usually ignore a show of knowledge and feign innocence of any wrongdoing. The interrogator must try not to reveal the extent of the information already possessed; but offer enough information to convince the person that admissions are in his own best interests, and what is being asked is already known. Experience has shown that certain techniques are generally applicable to any type of interrogation. So, while the desired outcome may vary, the interrogation techniques that are taught and employed represent a clearly defined body of knowledge, applicable to almost any goal. One important difference between the criminal interrogation and the CI interrogation is the fact that, usually, the criminal subject has not been trained to resist interrogation and is usually unfamiliar with the techniques being used. It is very likely that the CI subject has been trained to resist interrogation and to recognize the various techniques that are being employed.

Interrogation of any sort is a battle of wits. The person being interrogated has facts that he wants to conceal, e.g. the fact that he committed a crime. In the CI interrogation, frequently the person is only suspected of an offense, and it may not even be a certainty that an offense has occurred. The criminal interrogation is usually the result of a known offense and a logical suspect has been developed. The OSI instructors taught various techniques that have proven to be successful. An understanding of the facts and an appreciation of the type of personality that is the subject of the interrogation are absolute requirements for success.

Observation and Description was another interesting subject taught at the school. A system known as the "Portrait Parle," consisting of numerous plastic sheets, each containing different facial features and other physical characteristics was used. By changing the interrelationship of the sheets of plastic, different descriptions could be created. For example, a man with frontal baldness and small eyes could be created by changing the various pieces of plastic which individually contained mouths, eyes, hairlines, etc. It was a useful system, which I never saw again after I left the school.

Probably the most important subject taught was *Report Writing*. Though its importance was not particularly emphasized, no AFOSI agent could be successful if he was a poor report writer. An agent was absolutely judged by his ability to put on paper the results of his investigative effort. It seemed to be a universal that almost every agent lost interest in the case after it was solved and the report was due. In later years, when I became a supervisor of agents, I recognized how important the report was. If there was ever any criticism of investigative effort it would almost always be in connection with the poor or late reporting of the results. Instruction in report writing was excellent, but not as appreciated as it would be later, when the students were in the field and had to write proper and complete reports. It turned out to be one of those subjects that was not very glamorous, but its mastery was absolutely essential to the success of an agent. I tried to master the terse "nothing-but-the-facts" style of FBI reporting. It would take time.

The last subject taught was *Background Investigations* (BI). This type of investigation examined the life and experiences of people who possessed, or needed to possess a security clearance. Such a clearance allowed a person access to classified information. The information was classified as "Confidential," "Secret," or "Top Secret." In order to be accepted by OSI, we had to have a favorable BI. We learned how to assemble a complete picture of a person's life, sometimes from birth to the present. The basic tool of the Personnel Security Investigation, or the "PSI," as we called it, was the Personal History Statement. This consisted of numerous pages and sections dealing with a person's education, their work experience, social activities, and anything else that was pertinent for determining their loyalty and suitability for a clearance.

The Personal History Statement was the skeleton that, when fleshed out, gave the US Government a pretty complete picture of the person who was the subject. It revealed many obvious things that would disqualify a person. For example, prior arrests, or severe physical or psychological problems would usually be detected during police and medical checks, which were all part of the overall BI. Many people have criticized the BI as being an ineffective tool for determining the loyalty and suitability of a person.

As part of the BI, the investigator would ask a number of references to identify other people who knew the subject. Those identified were called "throw-offs." They were people who knew the subject, perhaps better than some of those given as references, but who were not given as references. Sometimes, though infrequently, these "throw-offs" would provide information not divulged by the subject and unknown by the references used. Interviewing additional references sometime revealed membership in subversive or anti-American political and social organizations. Police and other agency checks where the subject had lived or worked sometimes brought out arrest records that disqualified a subject.

Years later I would work with British Intelligence and discover that they did not pay sufficient attention to BIs. This could be the reason that they were so easily and completely penetrated by disloyal Britons who were agents of the Soviet Union. I doubt if any nation places the emphasis on the BI that the US does. Such investigations are extremely time-consuming and expensive. Since they are the least exciting types of investigation, many agents were not as thorough as they might be, and some were poorly accomplished. Only a very small percentage of people were denied positions or became the subject of investigation as a result of the BI. These were people though, whose unsuitability was very obvious.

The cost-effectiveness of BIs has long been a subject that has been hotly debated. I think that the question misses the point. Perhaps, one should ask whether or not we could afford not to have complete BIs on those who we entrust with secret sensitive information. The BI may not detect the hidden sympathies of an individual, but it will bring to light any overt activities that would preclude the person from gaining access to classified information.

Later in my career, the responsibility for PSI was given to a Defense Investigative Service (DIS), set up for that purpose. As far as I know, there has always been a backlog of these investigations and there probably is today. The foot-dragging of requesters has, to a great extent, been the cause of such tardiness. Addressing this matter is a command responsibility. Because of the lack of concern, it appears that a high priority is not given to the completion of these investigations. Many people, many as high as the White House have performed their duties and gained access before any BI on them was completed.

After completing agent school, I remained in the Washington, DC area and was involved in the conduct of PSIs. My investigations took me all over the area and they included northern Virginia and part of Maryland. In most instances, the people were courteous and cooperative because they were friends and wanted to help that person get a clearance. Some of the "throw-offs," whose names were developed from given references, were sometimes not as positive about the loyalty and suitability of the subject. This was undoubtedly the reason why they had not been given as references in the first place.

After a few months I was feeling quite confident about my ability as an investigator; at least as far as PSIs were concerned. One incident occurred that really diminished my self confidence. I had an interview at the National Security Agency (NSA) which was located at Fort Meade, Maryland. I was told at the gate that I could not enter the facility, but that they had a building at the entrance which could be used for interviews. I was advised to proceed there and that the reference, who was a young woman, would be sent out for the interview. I observed that there was no one else in the little building and waited dutifully for the reference to appear.

Shortly after I entered the building, a young woman appeared at the entrance and smiled warmly at me. I immediately showed her my AFOSI credentials, and began to ask her about the person who had given her as a reference. To my surprise, she stated that she did not know that person. I asked her numerous questions about her own history in an effort to connect her with the subject of the investigation. Nothing matched. Finally, I said, "Weren't you given as a reference by so-and-so?" and she responded, "No, I am the singer with the band that performed here at the Officer's Club over the weekend and I was told that if I came to this building someone would pay me." I apologized profusely and mentioned something to her about a bureaucratic foul-up. As she left, another young woman appeared at the building. After my cautious and very business-like introduction, she acknowledged that she did know the subject and would be happy to recommend him for a position of trust with the US Government. Since that was the last interview of the day, a privately embarrassed OSI agent headed back to the office.

As I reflected on my forthcoming assignment, I realized that I had received practically no instruction in CI.

Perhaps unfairly, I felt that this was the result of FBI influence on the curriculum. The many readings that I had done at the school library, where there was a vast amount of CI material, showed me that the AFOSI School sent agents into the field totally unqualified in even the basics of CI; this seemed to me to be a real weakness in the AFOSI training. I knew that the FBI had gained its reputation by conducting highly publicized criminal investigations. AFOSI was following suit and great emphasis was placed on criminal investigations.

To be fair, the FBI influence in AFOSI criminal investigations training was positive. It was thorough and highly professional. Most AFOSI agents who had completed the Basic Agent Course were able to conduct a simple criminal investigation with successful results.

The same could not be said of those same agents who attempted to conduct CI operations. This has led the theoreticians to conclude that "Law enforcement techniques that work against criminals seldom work against spies." Many practices and procedures used in criminal investigations are vital to successful CI investigations. For example surveillances are often used in CI investigations, as are photography, surreptitious searches, developing informants, as well as using open sources of information. I could not agree that criminal investigative experience did not help in CI investigations. I felt that the excellent training in criminal work would help me when I did get involved in CI work.

Shortly thereafter, I was told that my BI days were over and that I was to be sent back to the OSI School to attend the Advanced Special Investigations Officer Course, which lasted two weeks. It was a great learning experience because most of the other students were officer agents who had been out in the field, actually conducting investigations other than PSIs. During the school, I received my orders for assignment to the OSI District located on Okinawa. Finally, I was going to practice the skills that I had learned, and who knew, maybe get involved in CI. I learned that the District, consisting of about forty people, was commanded by an experienced Lieutenant Colonel named Louis Kolb, who was well thought of in OSI.

Okinawa, which had been under Japanese control prior to World War II, was now under the control of the United States. Two USAF bases were located there (one at Kadena and the other at Naha). The main CI threat was from an anti-US organization called the Okinawan Peoples Party (OPP). This group wanted US departure from Okinawa and reversion to Japan. Its leader, Kamejiro Senaga, had once been elected mayor of Naha City, the capital, much to the irritation of the US. At the time, it was believed that the OPP had direct connections with the Japan Communist Party (JCP), but no intelligence could confirm this connection. OPP activities were monitored closely because of the belief that they represented a potential threat to US security on the island. AFOSI's CI effort involved attempting to determine the role of the OPP and its possible connection to the JCP. The OPP was very active in attempting to foment labor agitation, and sought to penetrate those labor unions on the island. Fortunately, the OPP had limited funds and only a small number of dedicated members.

The penetration and monitoring of the OPP presented some of the same problems that we find in the Middle East today (2004). It was comprised of ethnic Japanese, who spoke what is called an "exotic" language, difficult for Westerners to master; the organizational membership was all ethnic Japanese, and even surveillance was difficult because its location was in an all Japanese area. CI coverage had to be accomplished by using native Japanese as penetration agents. This meant relying mostly on the cooperation of people whose loyalty to the US was, at least, problematical. Despite these limiting factors, the US still had control of the island and operations could be conducted in relative safety. Penetration of terrorist cells today presents many of the same problems that we experienced then. The one difference – the OPP had never engaged in violence. The Middle East terrorists' main efforts involve violence.

It seemed obvious to me that an agent needed a good knowledge of the Japanese language, history, customs and traditions. Without the language capability, CI agents had to rely on the accuracy and trustworthiness of native interpreters and translators. This has been historically the main problem with US Intelligence and CI. Both the FBI and the CIA have failed to develop an intensive language capability. Even today, the FBI has a large backlog of Arabic documents that need translating that must wait on the limited FBI capability.

The CIA has similarly neglected foreign language capability, especially in the more difficult languages like Arabic, Farsi, Korean and other non-Western languages. I would become more aware of this failing after I had assumed CI duties. One could never be completely certain that the interpreter was accurate and competent. Throughout my career, I would seek language training. Unfortunately, after I acquired it, my skill was misused. After studying Italian for twenty six weeks, I was assigned to the UK. A colleague spent a full year studying Greek and was assigned to Alaska. These were but a few examples of the misuse of language trained agents.

Near the end of my career, while conducting a study for the Director AFOSI, I found that 68% of language trained agents were not sent to the country whose language they had studied. Such misuse of assets, both financial and manpower, cost the CI effort badly. The CIA was no more professional in its use of language trained personnel. When the Agency opened its station in Berlin, at the beginning of the Cold War, they did not have a Russian language trained case officer. (Note: The Berlin Operating Base (BOB), set up by the CIA in July, 1945, did not acquire a Russian linguist until 1947). Almost all their efforts to acquire agents, were compromised and known to the Soviets. I was unaware of these things as I prepared for my assignment to Okinawa. I looked forward with optimism as the time for my assignment drew near. I was to be assigned to a detachment of the Okinawa office which was composed of four agents, an administrative airman and two Okinawan interpreters/ translators. It was located about thirteen miles south of the District Headquarters. The main activity there was support for the 16th Fighter Squadron. I knew that the assignment would be interesting and challenging, and perhaps a very busy one. I was to learn CI the hard way through experience. Fortunately, we were dealing with, what had been, a non-violent organization and control of the environment was definitely by the United States. The limited size of the island made monitoring and control relatively easy.

THE AGENT GOES FORTH

Okinawa is a small island located south of mainland Japan in the East China Sea. It is about sixty miles long and eighteen miles wide, at its widest point. The capital city, Naha, is within a two hour flight to Tokyo, Taipei, Hong Kong, Seoul, Shanghai and Manila. Its central location gives it a high strategic value for military operations. It is now part of the Japanese Okinawa Prefecture, which consists of about 160 primary islands and occupies the southern half of the Ryukyu Archipelago. Okinawa is kept warm by a subtropical climate and maintains its warmth when further north, Japan is freezing. During the summer months it is covered with brilliant flowers, dazzling white beaches paralleled by stunning coral formations. Today (2004), it receives over three million tourists from all over the world.

To many, Okinawa is better known for being the site of the last battle between the US and Japan during the Second World War. During April, 1945, US troops launched a major attack on Okinawa, under the codename "Operation Iceberg." It was one of the most savage battles of the war; it cost the lives of over 12,000 Americans, over 90,000 Japanese soldiers, and almost 94,000 Okinawan civilians before US forces conquered it. Okinawa comprises a significant strike force that could reach anywhere in Asia, a fact that was not lost on the Soviet Union, communist China, and North Korea.

My assumption that I would proceed to the detachment at Naha was incorrect. I was informed by a major, that I was to remain at headquarters until I "had a chance to get my feet wet." My duties would involve criminal investigations with the guidance and assistance of one of the enlisted agents. I was told that he was a Technical Sergeant named Harry Ankenbrand.

When I met Agent Ankenbrand I realized that I had indeed been fortunate. He was a professional who appreciated my uncomfortable position and treated me with the greatest courtesy. He informed me with a smile, that I could call him "Harry." Despite this informality, he continued to call me "Mr." until after a few weeks I asked him to call me by my first name. We worked well together; and I felt that I was getting guidance from one of the most professional agents on Okinawa. Events would confirm this feeling.

After a few weeks, Harry pretty much let me roam freely. His suggestions were always helpful. For example, the base was faced with a series of thefts from the airmen's dormitories. Watches, radios, wallets, and jewelry, anything left unattended disappeared. Harry told me that this was an easy one. I admitted that I could not see the case as being that simple. His experience came through for me, when he asked me why these thefts were taking place. I assumed that the thieves were selling the items. "Close" he said. "It is quicker to pawn the stuff off-base. Every pawnbroker must get a description of the item pawned, the name of the individual pawning it, and a thumb print from the individual entered in his pawn book. Just go downtown with your interpreter and check the pawnshops for the items that were stolen." I could not believe that it would be that easy. Energized by what I thought would be an easy investigation, I took my interpreter and headed for the nearest village.

After going to about ten pawnshops, without any results, I was tired, sweaty and somewhat discouraged. Late in the afternoon I entered what I decided would be my last pawnshop for the day. I asked, through my interpreter, to examine the pawn book. The second item I examined was a wristwatch. It fitted the description of one of the items stolen. Very helpfully, the person who pawned it gave his name and address. The address was one of the dormitories that had been hit hard by the wave of thefts. Reading further down the book, I found another item, which had been reported stolen. Another airman pawned it whose address was the same as the first one. I confiscated the items and returned in triumph to the base.

Harry was pleased to see that I had the aggressiveness to trudge around all day in the hot sun. He informed me that the case was only partly finished. Confessions from the two airmen were next in order. He suggested that I wait until the next day and call them both early in the morning and as he said, "Have a little chat with them." My joy turned to apprehension, as I contemplated my first criminal interrogation. I notified the First Sergeant that I wished to see the two airmen the next morning at the AFOSI Office.

Early the next day, Harry advised that he would sit in to help me, but it was my interrogation. He had suggested that I call them in at about 08.30 A.M. and let them sit for at least an hour, in the reception room. During that time, he discussed some ideas with me. First, he pointed out that these airmen were not likely to be professional criminals. They would be unlikely to resist interrogation, if it was done properly. "Always let them give you whatever explanation they want, the first time.

Then on the second run through, point out the discrepancies in their stories. They will usually respond to kindness and consideration."

I seated the first suspect, while leaving the second one out in the waiting room. I asked him if he needed a drink of water or desired to go to the restroom. After advising him of his constitutional rights, I discussed them with him and ensured that he understood them, carefully noting on my interview log the date, time and location of the advisement. Then I told him what I was investigating and that I would like to ask him a few questions, if he didn't object. I told him that I thought he could be very helpful to our investigation. I then focused on the other airman, who was waiting in reception. I asked him if he knew the fellow and were they friends. I then told him that we had discovered some stolen property, which had been pawned by the other airman. I also mentioned that they were known to be friends.

He immediately became flustered and said that he didn't know anything about the other fellow's activities. I said that we had definitely identified the other airman by his signature in the pawn book, in connection with the pawning of stolen property. Then calling him by his first name, I asked him if he wanted to talk about the situation.

He suddenly burst into tears and confessed that he and his friend were the ones who had been stealing from the dormitories. He wanted to know what would happen to him. I said that I didn't know, but I would mention that he had been cooperative with me. I asked him for a statement, detailing all that he had done. He agreed to prepare one, in his own handwriting. I provided with the forms necessary to execute a statement and again advised him of his rights and noted such on the form. He was told to take his time and tell the truth; to identify all the items and money that he had stolen, as best he could remember.

I left him alone in the interview room and then took his friend, who by then was frantic with fear, into another interview room. I immediately advised him of his constitutional rights and asked him to tell me about the thefts that he and his friend had been engaged in. Without hesitation, he detailed their activities and listed most of what had been stolen. Once again, I provided him with the forms, explained what we wanted from him. After satisfying myself that they had properly confessed to the thefts, I took their statements from them and released them to report to their First Sergeant. Both young airmen were extremely relieved after confessing their guilt. They would not be so happy after they talked to a lawyer. Not long after the interviews with the two airmen, they were court martialed and each of them received a bad conduct discharge.

After briefly testifying about the facts and circumstances surrounding their confessions, I was dismissed and left with a feeling of sadness that I could not explain. When I told Harry, he said that an agent should always feel a little sadness after getting information that led to a person's downfall. I continued to conduct criminal investigations at headquarters for about two months. All were relatively simple and successful.

I was called into Colonel Kolb's office and he told me that he was very pleased with my performance and that I was ready to report to Naha Air Force Base to work at the detachment there. He said that the commander, Special Agent Brewer Newton would assign me my duties. I took that opportunity to tell the colonel that I wished to get involved in CI. He said that an enlisted agent who would be returning soon to the United States was handling the CI Program at the detachment. Of course, it would be up to Brewer Newton as to whether or not I assumed the CI mission at the detachment. Colonel Kolb concluded by wishing me luck and telling me that Brewer Newton was an outstanding officer and that I was lucky to begin my career working for him.

I arrived at the detachment office on Naha Air Force Base and asked to see Mr. Newton. I was told by a person in civilian clothes that Mr. Newton was consulting with the Base Commander and would return soon. When I introduced myself, the person introduced himself as one of the agents assigned to the detachment. Another person emerged from the rear of the office and introduced himself. I recognized the second man as the one who was then handling the CI Program at Naha. He said that I would be briefed on the detachment caseload and the CI Program. When I told him that I was interested in getting into CI work he said that if that was my wish, with Mr. Newton's approval, he would start turning work over to me. Of course, that would be up to Mr. Newton. His exuberance was noticeable when I mentioned that I wanted to do CI work. He undoubtedly saw an opportunity to rid himself of that responsibility. He did not show much enthusiasm for CI work and stated that he preferred criminal investigations over CI work.

Shortly, Brewer Newton returned to the office. He immediately welcomed me to the detachment and took me into his office to find out if I was getting settled in. Without any hesitation, he said that he would be happy to put me into the CI Program. He said that there would not be any problem with my starting to assume the handling of the one good source that the detachment had. He explained that the agent who was handling Saito (not a true name) was leaving and would be happy to rid himself of the responsibility. I immediately liked Newton. He was professional, and very much in command. He also wanted to get the CI Program off the ground and felt that our informant, Saito, could be the means of doing that.

After a thorough briefing by Newton, I was briefed by the agent I was relieving as case officer for Saito. OSI referred to its sources as "informants," whereas what OSI would call an "informant," CIA would describe as an "agent." There could be some confusion from the different usage of these terms. Once again, OSI followed the FBI terminology pretty closely. According to the departing agent, Saito had been developed as an informant as a result of a criminal investigation by AFOSI. Saito was a witness and was extremely cooperative with AFOSI. The AFOSI agent who handled the case developed Saito, first as a criminal informant. But, when the agent found out that Saito was acquainted with the leading leftist on the island, Kamejiro Senaga, it was decided to target the subversive group by using Saito as a penetration agent against the OPP. Saito, upon being so instructed, joined the subversive organization and attended meetings, as a low-level member. The departing agent informed me that Saito was always met during the daytime. When asked why the meetings were not in the evening, to offer less chance of compromising Saito, the agent informed me that evenings were for his family. He did not work evenings, if he could avoid it. At all meetings, the agent was accompanied by an interpreter, who translated what Saito said. Whoever met with Saito had to rely completely on the interpreter. I asked when the interpreter had been polygraphed (slang for given a lie detector test). I was informed that it had been over two years. I decided that before I met with Saito, the interpreter would be polygraphed. Also, all meetings would be during evening hours. I became immediately aware of one OSI shortcoming, a dearth of language trained agents. Lacking in language capability, we had to rely on foreign interpreters whose efficiency and loyalty might be questionable. With some misgivings, I prepared for my first meet with Saito. I requested that my true name not be used and I informed the interpreter that I would be "Mr. Thomas" to Saito.

Prior to the first meet, I determined that Saito was paid only $20.00 per month and that there had been no raises given, although Saito had performed well over the year. I immediately sought and got a $5.00 raise for Saito, which began immediately. Saito would be informed of my raise at the first meeting. In 1957, the Okinawan wage scale was extremely low. A full-time interpreter was paid about $56.00 per month. In spite of this wage scale, I felt that Saito might be in some danger and another $5.00 did not seem exorbitant. The raise was to be a reward for past services and hopefully, a small inducement to continue with us and perhaps increase efforts against the targeted group.

OSI, like all other intelligence agencies used what we called "commodities;" these were cigarettes and liquor. They were generally given to Okinawa police officials and other Okinawan bureaucrats who had been helpful to us at one time or another. I found out that informants were also eligible to receive these commodities. I immediately set aside two cartons of cigarettes and two bottles of bourbon, to be given to Saito at the first meet. Saito would be instructed to entertain members of the subversive organization and thus, hopefully, gain their confidence. I would later find that this small investment would gain great favor for Saito among the members of that group. Of course, Saito could explain the acquisition of those commodities by pointing out that they were readily available on the black market.

Prior to the meet, I asked the interpreter to select a few sites for our meeting and to take me to them, at our approximate meeting time, so that I could observe entrance and exit routes, and the approximate population density which would be present at that time. I mentally selected one of the sites, but did not inform the interpreter which one, so that he would have no knowledge of the meeting site until the actual time of the meet. I also made a mental note to prepare a detailed list, for my review, of personal details about Saito so that I could ask about the health and wellbeing of immediate family members. First, to make a show of knowledge and second, to personalize our new relationship. I queried the interpreter for that information, since I wished the departing agent to be completely cut-off from the operation as of the date I assumed responsibility for it. I found the interpreter helpful and eager to help me establish a rapport with Saito.

On the day of the first meet, I reviewed every rule of tradecraft (the procedures used to perform intelligence and CI tasks securely). I requested the other agent to perform a countersurveillance function for me to ensure that I was neither observed nor followed. He would simply follow me to the meet site and observe whether or not I was being followed. He would also remain near the site, at a discreet distance, to determine whether or not anyone was observing us. He made it clear that this had never been done before. I pointed out to him that it would be done for all future meets. He grudgingly agreed to perform the task and we arranged a signal system, using car lights to ensure that he could warn me of any surveillance that might take place. I vetoed the use of any horn signals, since car lights were commonplace, but the use of horns in that area would only attract attention. I realized that these necessary security procedures were very basic, but should always be employed.

Finally, I reviewed the operation with Brewer Newton and he seemed pleased that I had made a great effort to conduct this operation in a professional manner. It was during this discussion that I discovered that Newton was a qualified Japanese linguist. He spoke with the interpreter for a few minutes and asked him to help me as best he could. When I said that I didn't know that he was a linguist he replied that sometimes it was a good idea not to advertise a capability. He also gave me a shrewd piece of advice. He said that when working through an interpreter one should not assume the informant was ignorant of English, and not to say anything that you would not say to the person. Also, address all comments to the person and let the interpreter translate. Do not address the interpreter. Each meet should begin with a recap of all that has occurred to the informant since the last meet, emphasizing information acquired, security problems, possible sources of information encountered, and suggestions for future activities.

My first meeting with Saito was successful. We hit it off well and he freely discussed what had happened to him since the last meeting. It was clear to me that he was not used to being questioned in the detail that I had reached. He was pleased that we were now meeting at night. He had been apprehensive about meeting in the daylight, where he could possibly be observed by some of the subversives. He appeared surprised that I knew something about his family and seemed to appreciate my enquiring. I briefly discussed the possibility of getting him to advance to a higher position in the organization. I also mentioned that the use of cigarettes and whisky, provided by OSI, would help him to accomplish his advancement in the party. After the meeting, my interpreter told me that he had not seen Saito exhibit such enthusiasm before and he felt that Saito was going to actively try and reach the higher levels of the organization. It was a beginning.

For years, United States Counterintelligence had tried to determine if the local subversive organization had any direct ties with the JCP. Despite repeated attempts, the US could not penetrate the organization at a high enough level to determine if there was a direct connection. I decided that Saito was going to be our "penetration agent" who would reach a high enough level to find out just what ties existed between the two organizations. No ordinary member could achieve this level of penetration and Saito would have to reach the inner sanctum in order to acquire this information.

As weeks went by, Saito wined and dined the leadership of the subversive party and gradually became more involved in party activities and privy to information never before revealed to him. On one occasion he was told that the subversives were planning to set up a labor union among the taxi drivers on Okinawa. It was revealed to him that action against the Americans, in the form of economic warfare, would take place when the union became strong enough. Taxi drivers represented a significant part of the economy, which revolved around services provided to the US bases on Okinawa. All of the drivers had access to US bases and were able to enter anytime, day or night. Although the potential for sabotage did not appear very great, there was definitely a possibility of disruptive strikes and labor agitation.

Access to all the information relevant to its management, plans and activities, as well as the composition of its membership was the goal of the AFOSI. With this in mind, I sought to find someone who could assist us in this venture. We had developed a taxi driver who had been helpful in providing criminal information, mostly about black market activities. I arranged a secluded meeting with him and discussed the possibility of his helping us to gain detailed information about this union. He had the personality and intelligence that would make him an ideal agent. Unfortunately, he advised us that he was familiar with the union and he was ineligible to join because he owned his own taxi. Only men employed as drivers were eligible to join. He said that the subversives were aggressively recruiting drivers and had made no secret of the fact that the union would not be favorable to the US.

After some conversation, the fellow told us (my interpreter and me) that he employed a man that would make an ideal candidate for the mission. A driver named Saburo (not his true name) was working for him and needed some extra money in order to get married. He was pro-American, spoke excellent English and was very outgoing and personable. Within a short time we had a meeting with Saburo. Prior to the meeting, we had run his name through our files and found out that he had been arrested once, several years ago, for being drunk and disorderly. He had no other unfavorable information in his background. We did not run his name through the CIC that was operating on Okinawa. Our relations with that organization were extremely poor. The OSI Commander and the CIC Commander did not even speak to each other and, consequently, there was almost no liaison between the two organizations. Hence, there was no cooperation or exchange of information between them.

The CIC detachment had many more people engaged in CI than did the OSI. We knew, through a CIA Liaison Officer, that the CIC had been extremely unsuccessful in penetrating the subversives. In fact, they did not have an agent in the organization. I learned that the CIC detachment had several Nisei (Japanese Americans) who spoke Japanese. Despite this apparent capability they were unsuccessful. I was told that the Nisei agents were easily identified by the locals because of their American clothing, haircuts and the fact that they wore expensive wingtip shoes that were clearly of American origin. To my surprise, I was told that their command of the Japanese language was not that good and this identified them as non-native Japanese. I became determined to find out more about this feud between the two organizations, which decreased the efficiency of both.

Saburo was a natural agent. He had the personality and curiosity that made him want to excel at collecting information about the union. I spent several days meeting with him and giving him information and security practices that would prevent his being compromised. Actually, security was very much a personal matter with him. Since he was a taxi driver, he came into frequent contact with Americans and there was nothing suspicious about his being seen dealing with Americans, a significant advantage over Saito, who would have difficulty explaining any contact with Americans. His was what we called a "natural cover." He did not have to assume another identity and his everyday actions and contacts were well within his perceived lifestyle. He did not have to pretend to be anyone other than himself. He was a taxi driver seeking to join a taxi union. Such a cover would greatly facilitate a collection operation and lessen the chance for compromise. One important goal was to identify all of the taxi drivers who were officers and members of the union, and to find out what the union's specific goals were in relation to the US Government, and to collect biographic information on all officers and active members of that organization. This same Essential Element of Information (EEI) was also levied on Saito. He was to also get biographic information on all members of the subversive organization, particularly the leaders. We now had two informants who were in a position to provide information on the plans, activities and personnel of this subversive group whose goal was to deny the US any use of Okinawa as a forward base.

My attention turned back to the CIC detachment when Saito advised that the subversives had a list of five people who were living in the village outside Naha airbase and posing as Japanese. According to Saito, these people were clearly identified as agents of the CIC detachment. I immediately reported the information to District Headquarters and was told not to release this information to the CIC detachment. The purpose for limiting this information was to embarrass the CIC.

Brewer Newton and I had visited the CIC detachment a few times, and although treated courteously, we were never given any useful information. Both of us felt that the CIC Operations Officer, a major and a Nisei, desired to cooperate with us, but was not going to violate the unofficial policy of denying OSI any cooperation. I learned that CIC had many more resources than us at their disposal. They had surveillance equipment, listening devices, and experienced personnel, who, if allied with us, would present a formidable CI presence on Okinawa. I knew that the present lack of cooperation would continue unless someone ignored the unofficial policy and exchanged information. I did not feel that the CIC would go first.

I telephoned the CIC Operations Officer at his home, and set up a meeting, to his huge surprise. I told him that I had information from a reliable informant who, if revealed publicly, might be very embarrassing to CIC. I felt that the subversives would use it to discredit the CIC. I then revealed the addresses that I had been given. The memo I gave him could not compromise Saito. He was very pleased and said, with a smile, "A couple of these addresses are not ours." He asked why I had given him this information and I said that I was tired of the childish behavior of both our organizations and that I would like to make the first move in establishing an effective liaison with CIC. I said I would provide all the information that would be beneficial to the CIC, but I would not reveal any OSI informants.

As if I had pushed a button, the whole atmosphere changed. He then told me, "OK, here's my contribution." He asked if I knew about a CIA safe house that was being used by OSI agents from headquarters. I said that I did not. He advised that the CIC knew that it was being used by us and that it had been compromised months ago. In fact neighbors referred to it as the "CIA House." If the place was that well-known, there was a good chance that some of the subversives might become aware of OSI's use of this facility.

A "safe house" is a secure building, usually a residence, that can be used for clandestine meetings. It must be carefully selected and offer easy access without compromise. It provides a meeting place that is unaffected by the weather and usually has comfortable surroundings.

It can frequently be used for lengthy debriefings of agents. It may have tape recorders secretly installed for surreptitious recordings of conversations. If its connection with the operating agency becomes known to the opposition, it becomes worthless as a secure meeting place and must be abandoned. Merely by observing who entered and left and following them would reveal a great amount of information to any opposition members.

I knew I had to inform the OSI District Headquarters of the widespread knowledge about the CIA safe house. I also knew that I could not attribute the information to the CIC.

My interpreter suggested that we visit a local Okinawan police official, who had been somewhat helpful in the past. I was told to ask him directly about the safe house's ownership and whatever else he might know about it. I met with the official and asked him about the house. I explained that the house was rather prominent because of its size and its non-Japanese appearance. He immediately informed me that US Government owned it and that it was operated by the CIA. I was amazed and asked him the source of his knowledge. He said that his police officers had observed different people entering and leaving the house and that they took down license numbers and ran checks with the US Army Military Police. Most of the individuals observed were identified as being assigned to a base which everyone knew was a CIA facility.

I was also informed that several OSI vehicles had been observed entering and leaving the house. From all this, I knew that it was a simple matter to advise the AFOSI District Office of the compromised safe house and attribute the revelation to the Okinawan police. I asked the official why he had not informed us of this matter before. His reply was that he thought that all American agencies were aware of the house and its activities. He told me further that all non-Okinawans living in the villages were identified by the Okinawan police.

I made a mental note to tell my CIC friend that it might be time to bring the boys home, as their "under-cover" presence was very likely compromised. I assumed that my headquarters, when briefed, would inform the CIA of the situation. I briefed the OSI Headquarters and assumed that they would immediately brief the CIA. I found out months later that the CIA had not been briefed on any of the details surrounding the compromise of the safe house. The reason given me was that OSI might want to use the information as a bargaining tool in dealing with the CIA. It seemed that CIA was not particularly forthcoming in its dealings with OSI. I thought, "So much for inter-service cooperation."

To my surprise, the people at my headquarters were not particularly pleased at my revelation concerning the safe house. It turned out that some of the agents from headquarters were meeting criminal informants there. They were not involved in CI and some felt that the house could still be used. Impatiently, I pointed out that if they did not mind letting the Okinawan police know who their criminal informants were then they might still use the house. The answer received was that, "The Okinawans probably already know who our informants are."

From that incident I decided that, at least on Okinawa, I would not use a safe house and that if I had to use one, I would not use it more than once. I had been meeting in vehicles and was able to find parking places far removed from the population centers and had the ability to observe anyone entering the area. It was not perfect, but it had none of the disadvantages of a fixed dwelling that could be observed anytime by anyone. I also learned from the incident that the Okinawan police were more sophisticated than we gave them credit for, and that the CIA and, for that matter the OSI, may be less sophisticated than I thought.

The US Army controlled all travel to and from Okinawa. Theoretically, no one could enter or leave the island without the Army knowing about it. The CIC was monitoring these matters and was responsible for insuring that no subversive left the island for Japan without the CIC's knowledge. Also, if necessary, the CIC was to surveille anyone of interest from the time they went to Japan until they returned to Okinawa. Somehow, those identified as subversives were to be monitored, by CIC agents, when traveling.

Saito reported that a well-known subversive was secretly leaving for Japan and had no difficulty getting permission to travel from the US Army. It appeared that the CIC's coverage had failed to detect this. When I reported this to AFOSI Headquarters, I was informed that the Army had "screwed up" and would be embarrassed when the subversive left and returned without its knowledge. Once again, I contacted my friend at CIC, two days before the travel date, and advised him of the identity of the subversive, who had seemingly slipped through the net.

I was then advised by the CIC officer that he wanted to pass something along to me. He said that the CIC had picked up information that the subversives were using some of their most radical members to set up a labor union for the taxi drivers on Okinawa. He gave me the names of the known organizers and mentioned that one of them was particularly well-known as a member of the subversive organization. Among the names given me was that of Saburo, and CIC did not leave out the fact that he had been arrested once. Their information confirmed everything Saburo was telling us, but was not quite as detailed. They identified a building that had been rented for a union meeting place. Two days later, at a meet with Saburo, he told us, without being questioned, that the union had rented a building. He also provided me with a scaled drawing of the interior. Between the efforts of the OSI and the CIC, we were getting a detailed look at the formation of a subversive organization, from its beginning. This, without either organization knowing that they were unofficially working together.

On a few occasions, I would have Saburo followed after a meet. This was to determine whether or not he reported back to the subversives, and if he did meet with them, would he tell me about it at the next meet. He never did anything to suggest that he was working as a "double agent." That is, someone who ostensibly spies for one organization, but actually works for the organization that he is supposed to be spying on. The advantages of such a set-up are tremendous for the organization that the agent is loyal to. They become knowledgeable of what the opposition is interested in finding out and have a channel to feed disinformation to that opposing organization. During World War II, the British established what they called "The Double Cross" system. It involved using German spies, who had been apprehended, to transmit false and misleading information to German Intelligence. The operation successfully mislead the Germans into thinking that the invasion would take place in one area of France, when it took place in another. The benefits to be derived from using a good double agent can be limitless.

One danger in using double agents is the possibility of the opposition redoubling the agent. This may happen if he is found out and forced to change sides "or else." Another danger is the fact that someone who can be so duplicitous may not be safely considered trustworthy.

I felt confident that both Saito and Saburo were not working for the opposition. We now had two good informants targeted against them. My confidence was not unjustified. Saito rose higher in the party and started giving us high-level information about the plans and activities of the leading subversives. We were not only getting coverage on the new taxi driver's union, but Saburo was getting information from the person who was their labor union organizer. He would advise Saburo of meetings of the subversives that took place and we could often use that information to verify information offered by Saito. We still had a long way to go.

Hundreds of Americans, Filipinos, and Chinese business people lived on Okinawa and often traveled from Okinawa to Japan and Hong Kong. There was no doubt that these people had legitimate business enterprises which gave them the opportunity to travel off island frequently. They engaged in operating bookstores, importing food, bottling soft drinks, tailoring, and other business pursuits. Many of these people had frequent access to our military bases either through their business activities or as guests of military personnel. There were unlimited possibilities for the collection of intelligence information and we knew very little about most of these people. The information that they provided to our immigration service on Okinawa was sketchy.

I received, through base distribution, a free copy of a civilian magazine named *Okinawa This Month*. It was written for and about civilians living and working on the island. As I read it, I found out that it covered all of the social and business activities of the civilians that we were interested in knowing more about. Each month an article dedicated to one civilian business person gave a lengthy biography with a photograph of the individual. I saw in this an opportunity to use an "open source" to collect information on our civilian population.

An "open source" is a source of information readily available to anyone. Books, newspapers, directories, business advertisements, people who are openly contacted for information, such as police liaison contacts and publications like *Okinawa This Month* which provided a wealth of information about people and their business and social activities. When I mentioned this to my interpreter, he suggested that we get back copies of the publication and start a file on those civilians mentioned. I asked, "How can we get back copies of this publication?" He said, "My sister-in-law works there and can provide us with all the back copies we would need." He thought that perhaps there were as many as forty eight months of back copies available to us.

Two days later, my interpreter arrived with a shopping bag full of back issues of the publication. We counted out fifty two different issues of the magazine. That weekend, we cut and pasted and mounted on 8 x 5" cards all of the information provided by the publication. When we finished, late in the afternoon, we had a remarkable file, with an alphabetical index on over seventy people. We had good photographs of at least fifty of them. We also clipped brief references of when so and so went to Hong Kong or made a trip to Japan. Adverts appearing in the magazine gave business addresses, phone numbers, and the names of the owners and managers of many businesses. It took us less than a full day to set up a file on a large number of people who had previously been relatively unknown. We also indicated on their file those who had regularly traveled off-island to Japan, Taiwan, Hong Kong and Korea. A few people in our file spent a great amount of time traveling to those places. All of this travel was unmonitored and completely uncontrolled. The opportunity for intelligence activity was unlimited and their access to the US bases gave them the opportunity to collect military information.

We were seldom visited by anyone from CIA, unless they wanted something from us. They rarely made a visit to us just for the purpose of liaison. Shortly after we began our file, a CIA officer came to our office and asked us what we knew about a certain civilian living on the island. With my fingers crossed, I produced this file box and asked him for a correct spelling of the person's name. Luck was with us. I found not only a biographic article, but several references to his trips on and off the island. I offered the file to the CIA person, but told him that he could only copy it. We did not release any of our files. I told him that if he wanted a copy of the picture of the individual we could have it copied and send it to him. He made some comment about the file being really comprehensive. With a straight face, I opened the file box and asked him his full name. After I enjoyed his look of surprise and mild apprehension, I told him that I was only kidding. He did not seem completely convinced that we didn't have a file on him. He had no idea where we got the information. That was "open source" research at its best.

Another source of concern regarding CI was the possibility of our military people being targeted off-base and asked questions about the base and their duties. OSI had the responsibility for giving periodic defensive intelligence briefings to USAF personnel. When I asked, I found that no briefings had been given for over a year. We set up a CI briefing, to be given to all base personnel, in the base theater. We emphasized the fact that seemingly innocent questions could result in detailed information about personnel, equipment, and activities. I expanded this program to include the US Marines, who were stationed on Okinawa. They were a particularly receptive audience.

Though it was not classified, we had security police at all the entrances to give the presentation an air of importance. Brewer Newton gave the presentation and did an excellent job of inspiring personnel to be more security conscious. We felt that, at least for a while, if any of our people were questioned, by anyone, they would report it to us.

The US Marine Company was assigned to Naha airbase and the captain who commanded it advised me that they had not been invited to the briefing. I set up and gave a special briefings to the Marines. I never saw a more responsive group of young men. Like their captain, they epitomized the "Gung Ho" attitude that is typical of the Marines. We included the Marines in all our briefings, but gave them a separate briefing from our Air Force personnel. The briefings described how information could be gained from them without their being aware of it and they should report to us any attempts by anyone to gain information about them or their duties. Thereafter, we received many reports from individual Marines who felt that they had been questioned too much about their mission. This close liaison with the Marines would pay off sooner than I expected.

In the spring of 1960, President Eisenhower visited Japan and was jeered and demonstrated against by the Japanese. As he finished his visit to Japan we were notified that he was going to visit Okinawa. At the next meet, I queried Saito about any plans that the subversives might have for our President. He had heard nothing. Two days later, I got a call, on the unlisted telephone in our office. It was always answered in Japanese by my interpreter. Saito wanted an emergency meeting for that evening and we agreed. The telephone allowed any of our informants to call us during any workday to arrange immediate contact should it be desired. Only the interpreters engaged in assisting in CI work were allowed to answer the telephone.

Saito had spoken to one of the high level subversives

and she had told him that they were planning a hot reception for President Eisenhower. According to Saito, every subversive was going to turn out for a mass demonstration against the President when he arrived in Naha City. When his automobile pulled up in the government complex, it was to be surrounded by two groups of demonstrators, each converging from adjacent streets. They were to be directed by high-level subversives who, using bullhorns, would control the demonstrators and order them to surround the presidential motorcade. They would be carrying Japanese flags, which they would be provided with just prior to the demonstration. It was against the law to display Japanese flags on Okinawa at that time. There was no indication that any violence was planned, but violence could easily occur, if they got close enough to the motorcade.

I immediately notified the District Headquarters at Kadena airbase. I was assured that the information would be immediately passed to the Secret Service in Japan, prior to the President's departure for Okinawa. I was told not to pass this on to the CIC. Because of the seriousness of this information and the order not to pass it to the CIC, I did not forward it to them. I assumed that we at Naha would be contacted by the advance Secret Service agents who always preceded the President. I heard nothing. I contacted my headquarters and they assured me that the information had been passed to the Secret Service and that they had received no reply or instructions from them. I asked what the Secret Service had been told. According to one of the administrative sergeants, the Secret Service had only been told to expect small anti-American demonstrations when the President came to Naha City. I understood why the Secret Service had not responded. They expected and had encountered demonstrations throughout the President's trip. The Secret Service had not been alerted to the possibility of violence.

I realized that the President would arrive soon, that there had been no steps taken to protect him against any crowd violence, should it occur. I contacted the Marine captain and told him of the problem. He asked me to take him to the square where President Eisenhower would arrive and brought his Sergeant Major with him. He made some notes, confirmed the times and was given a complete briefing on just where the subversives and those sympathetic to them, would enter the square and surround the motorcade. He then asked me if I could have a helicopter available. I told him that it would be easy to get one of my pilot friends in the Air Rescue Squadron to oblige.

I was in the square when the President's motorcade arrived the next day. Just as Saito had advised, demonstrators emerged from the two streets adjacent to the government buildings. They had not yet reached the square, when from the bottom floor of the main government building came about fifty US Marines, carrying rifles with covered bayonets. They broke up into two formations and proceeded to force the demonstrators back from the square. Almost at once, a USAF helicopter came down and landed in the square. The Secret Service, as professional as ever, quickly took the President from his car and hustled him into the helicopter. It disappeared in seconds and spirited him back to Kadena airbase, where he would be safe. Later I asked my commander to sign a letter of thanks to the Marine captain and his men. I asked that it be sent to the captain's commander for presentation. I heard no more about the matter or the letter.

Not long after the incident involving the President, Saito reported that one of the leading subversives had obtained employment at an American firm. It was his intention to try and organize a labor union. He had used his true name in obtaining the employment and the only other information that we had was that it was a large business, employing many Okinawans. There were only a few large American businesses on Okinawa, so we began an examination of each of them. Our search focused on a soft drink bottling plant, which was one of only two or three on the island. I went directly to the owner of the plant and explained exactly what we were trying to do to counter a threat that he might have to face. He said that he had never had any labor problems and that all his employees were loyal. I asked him to check and see if he had hired anyone within the last three months. A check by the owner revealed that he had hired three or four people. He produced a list of names and our subversive was on the list. We asked that no action be taken until we decided on a plan of action and the owner agreed.

By this time, Brewer Newton had just departed for the US, and as the next ranking agent, I assumed command of the detachment at Naha. Since I only had three months remaining on my tour, my replacement, an experienced agent named Andrew Smith, arrived and was detained at headquarters until I was ready to leave. He came down to the detachment to meet me and immediately told me that he was strictly a CI man and that he spoke Japanese. We hit it off splendidly and I asked him to come down when he could and maybe we could get something more going in CI. He started spending a lot of time at the detachment. I briefed him on the incipient labor union at the American business. We agreed to work together to formulate a plan of action concerning this latest threat from the subversive element on Okinawa.

I introduced him to the owner of the business and the three of us discussed the situation in detail. The owner asked how many other businesses were facing the same potential labor problem. We all agreed that there was no way of knowing. We then theorized that what if all the American owners were to exchange information with each other and advise each other of the identities of any actual or potential labor agitators. We would provide the names of any subversives suspected of working for American firms who may be engaged in labor agitation.

This plan was submitted to our headquarters and we were told that since it involved non-Air Force American civilians, it would have to be cleared with the CIA. A few weeks later we were told that such an operation was beyond OSI's mission and that it would not be "politically expedient" for us to engage in labor activities. That was the end of our efforts in that area of operations.

Saburo was rapidly advancing in the taxi drivers' union. He was given keys to their union hall and was there constantly. At one meet, he asked if we were interested in obtaining a membership roster of the union. Overjoyed, I asked him how this could be achieved. He said that on an evening when he was the only person there he could get access to the book for a few hours, if we wanted to copy it. He warned that we would only have a couple of hours. We set up a meet and Saburo arrived with the membership book.

To my horror, it was almost two hundred pages.

There was no way that we could copy it in just a couple hours. Desperate, I called my CIC friend. He asked me to have the book at their office as soon as possible and it would be taken care of. I arrived within minutes, as we were not too far away. I was immediately taken into a room that had a large camera setup. It could photograph four pages at once. Within one and half hours, Saburo had removed the book, had it copied and replaced it. We had gotten the complete membership roster with all the personal information for each union member. All I had to do was justify sharing it with the CIC.

When I explained to our headquarters that it was either allow the CIC to copy it for us or not get it copied at all, I was grudgingly told that I had done the right thing. Of course, the CIC took a while to give us the copied book; but it was translated for our benefit. This saved our people a lot of translation time. When the roster was sent to OSI Headquarters in Washington, DC, we were given high praise and I was singled out as having been responsible for the operation. I realized that the credit belonged to Saburo, who, on his own initiative, set the whole operation up and ensured its success. The operation gave me a chance to introduce my replacement to the CIC. He was well received, especially since during his earlier career he had been a CIC agent. He assured me that he would maintain the same "clandestine" relationship with the CIC that I had.

Colonel Kolb returned to the United States and Colonel William L. Mann replaced him. Colonel Mann was young, intelligent, professional, and dedicated to CI. He had been told about my efforts in CI and gave me the first real recognition. He shared with me his plans for CI operations on Okinawa and I was almost sorry to be leaving. Working for him would have been a great experience. He was very accomplished in technical matters and desired to develop a professional visual and audio-surveillance capability for OSI world-wide. He also planned to aggressively seek opportunities for CI operations. One of the first things that he did was make a courtesy call on the CIC Commander and pledge full cooperation. If anyone could cement relations with the CIC, or any other US agency, Colonel Mann could, and he started doing just that. He also recommended me for a Commendation Medal, an honor rarely given junior officers in OSI at that time.

When Colonel Mann arrived on Okinawa, I only had a few months left on my thirty month tour. I felt that I had learned a lot about CI and had accomplished a few worthwhile things. I planned to carry out a couple of other projects which I turned over to my replacement. I became aware that every time one of our agents went into a city or village he was instantly recognizable as being non-Japanese. If he spent any length of time there, in order to familiarize himself with the area, he became even more noticeable. There was a reconnaissance squadron located at Kadena airbase. Photo reconnaissance was their business.

I planned to have an aerial mosaic made of the entire island. It would be at a scale of 1:5000. Every building, footpath, and road would be clearly visible. Places could be examined without actually going to their location. I met a Master Sergeant who was a photographic specialist and he said he could put the mosaic together if he had the proper photographs and supplies. At a scale of 1:5000, everything on the island would be in sharp detail. After discussing this with him, I contacted the reconnaissance squadron's Operations Officer and requested the photographic mission. The result was several large rolls of developed film with 9 x 9" negatives, which would enlarge to show fantastic detail. The final project would be a 5 x 8' photo mosaic. By appending a plastic overlay, marking could be made on it. The hitch was the fact that the sergeant worked for a particularly uncooperative officer who insisted that this extra project be done on the sergeant's own time. The sergeant was eager to accomplish the task and proceeded to work on the layout of the huge pictorial map whenever he could. The project was about half completed when I had to return to the United States.

Another project involving photography was undertaken by me in response to the CIC. In the event that an emergency was declared, there were certain people who would be immediately detained by the CIC. It was necessary to locate their residences and quickly apprehend them. Most of these people lived in or near Naha City. The address system was a jumble of pre-World War II, World War II, and recent changes to both. Finding anyone's residence strictly from the address would be a very difficult task for a native of the island and an impossible one for anyone else.

Located in the city center was a large movie theater named the Kakuai Khan. From the air any specific location could be located in relation to it. First, we went in on the ground, and to those places that we were interested in photographing, I used interpreters and their wives or girlfriends. They carried Japan Airline bags along with their cameras. In three days, with an expenditure of about one hour each day, we had photographs of the top fifteen subversives' homes. The photography was done during the day, when most Okinawans were working. We followed up on the ground photos by photographing the homes from a helicopter, at 1000 feet. When the project was complete, we presented a briefing to Colonel Mann. He was very pleased the aerial shots could easily be related to the position of the individual homes relative to the theater. This system would allow anyone to locate the residences in a very short time. The project was made using 35 mm color slides which would enlarge to show great detail.

Colonel Mann asked that we give the briefing again the next day. When we returned to present the briefing; my friend the Major and his CIC Commander were present in the briefing room. We presented the complete briefing again and both the major and his commander were silent but obviously very interested. When the briefing was complete, Colonel Mann presented to the CIC Commander a complete copy of the briefing. It was a rewarding moment. The formality that had existed between OSI and the CIC seemed to disappear. Both the commander and the major expressed their thanks for this outstanding contribution to their mission. There were expressions from both sides, and assurances that there would be full cooperation in the future. I believe that Colonel Mann had made it happen.

Colonel Mann kept me working right up until I was to leave. We gave the color slide briefing to the USAF Wing Commander, a General. He was greatly impressed with the presentation. The colonel pointed out that this was a joint project and the CIC would actually be responsible for the detaining of those people on a special list while OSI had assisted them in putting together a program to facilitate the apprehension and detention of those selected. As the list of those to possibly be detained in an emergency changed, OSI would work with the CIC to ensure its completeness and accuracy. If it worked, it would be an outstanding example of how the two organizations could work together for a common purpose. I felt that the only thing that could work against the program's success was the reemergence of inter-service rivalry.

Thirty months had passed since I arrived on Okinawa. During that time, I had worked at developing informants to monitor the subversive element. Progress had been made in developing an informant who could keep us apprised of their most secret activities. I learned through experience how to target opposition elements and how to develop informants to accomplish that purpose. I became aware of the basic elements of tradecraft. That is, those practices and procedures which ensure the security of CI operations. Things that I recognized as truisms in CI were the need for language capability, the great rewards to be derived from working closely with organizations such as the CIC, the importance of knowing thoroughly the geographic area within which we were working, and the continuous search for additional resources needed to closely monitor the subversive element. Such efforts, if successful, would deny the subversive element its goal of embarrassing the United States and deny it the use of a group of forward bases, such as those on Okinawa.

It was true that I had been very fortunate to have begun my CI career in a place where the United States exercised strict control. Because of it, there was little threat of violence. We operated from the safety and security of our bases against an element that, though equally dedicated, was lacking in any effective organizational structure and equally lacking in sufficient funds to carry out many plans that they might conceive. It had been almost a laboratory situation. The lessons learned were, nevertheless, lasting, important and applicable to many other situations requiring effective CI. My new assignment was to the OSI Headquarters in Washington, DC, in the CI Division. It was a great surprise to me and unheard of for a junior officer in OSI to be given such a responsible assignment.

I reported to headquarters in October in 1960. Washington was at its best in October and the weather was beautiful. I looked forward to my new assignment and the experiences it would bring.

RUNNING THE "SPECIALS"

When I reported in to the OSI Headquarters, known by its inhabitants as "The Directorate," I immediately became aware of the lack of any frantic activity. The people who worked in the various divisions seemed to resemble civilian bureaucrats more than the field personnel that I had worked with. It made me feel a little guilty to realize that there was seldom any overtime and people always had the time to discuss personal and professional matters. Everyone wore civilian clothes and there was an air of casualness pervading the whole organization. It was quickly pointed out to me by members of the CI Division that I was now a member of the OSI Headquarters staff. This was the organizational element that supervised worldwide field operations.

To accomplish the task of worldwide supervision the Directorate was divided into several divisions. The organizational structure resembled that of any intelligence or CI organization that might be found anywhere in the world. Both our friends and enemies had organizational structures defined by the functions that they were to carry out. The CI Division, to which I had been assigned, consisted of branches. There was the Counterespionage Branch, whose job it was to supervise all the counterespionage operations conducted by OSI throughout the world. These would include espionage cases, investigations to determine if a person or group was spying against the United States; double agent operations, which were operations designed to introduce an

OSI asset into the service of a foreign intelligence organization, either as a result of contact with a foreign intelligence service or as a result of placing the asset in position to be approached by foreign intelligence. There was the Internal Security Division which investigated matters of loyalty and suitability in connection with USAF members and employees. The Analysis and Dissemination Branch (A&D) consisted of CI analysts, assigned to cover geographic areas of the world. For example, the Pacific Air Force (PACAF) Branch was responsible for analyzing all CI reports emanating from the Far East, e.g. Japan, Taiwan, Korea, and the Philippines.

My assignment was to the Special Activities Branch which was responsible for activities of special interest to the Director, who commanded OSI, though he was physically located in the Pentagon. He was a Brigadier General, usually a military academy graduate, who was either on his way up or out of the Air Force. I was informed that the present Director was a General who was close to retirement. I questioned whether or not people, who were "just passing through" would be that interested in OSI and its activities. Later, I would find that my apprehensions were not without foundation.

Most of the people in the USAF were not familiar with OSI and few had direct contact with it. They did not understand the CI mission of OSI and thus had little knowledge or interest in it. Those who were familiar with OSI were usually those who had become involved in criminal investigations, either as subjects or witnesses. They were reluctant to have any dealings with OSI if they could avoid it. Unlike the FBI, who sought good publicity anytime they could get it, OSI remained largely an enigma. This relative anonymity was a double-edged sword. It allowed OSI to operate unnoticed and unimpeded, but because of this anonymity it received little cooperation and support from the Air Force as a whole, particularly in the CI area.

Shortly after I had reported in, I was called in to the Division Chief and told that I was going to be project officer on a "special." He explained that the US Secret Service was undermanned and needed assistance in protecting Distinguished Visitors (DVs) and occasionally the President and other high ranking US officials. This was particularly true when they traveled to USAF installations. I was to coordinate with the Secret Service and receive all the training material that they could make available concerning protection coverage activities. I was then to write an OSI "Bulletin" that would be used to train OSI agents, so that they could participate in those operations.

I was given free reign to contact any agency that might be helpful in providing the necessary information. The project continued for several months and no one tried to speed up my efforts. The Secret Service was the most helpful in providing planning and operational techniques. I received nothing from the FBI or the CIA.

The result of my efforts was an OSI Bulletin which discussed the concept of protection coverage of DVs. Key in such operations were: planning, preparation and concentration. The idea of concentric rings of safety emanating from the DV was the essential strategy. Depending on the nature of the threat, the location of the DV and the time element involved, the rings should extend out as far as possible. For example, the innermost ring was where the DV was located; coverage in that area should be as complete as possible. No one can enter that inner ring unless cleared and identified. As the rings extend outward, control is reduced and coverage can be effected by three entities; guard personnel, people whose only job is to stop anyone from entering the ring that they control and reporting any breaches of security; locking devices, and anti-intrusion devices, such as alarms and video designed to warn of entry into an area. Depending on the place and circumstances, some or all of these devices may be used. All must be frequently monitored by personnel to ensure that there has not been a breach or a device neutralized.

Of particular concern is the innermost ring. It must be large enough to prevent would be attackers from getting close enough to the DV. Anything in that area must be inspected and then closely controlled. For example, food and cooking utensils must be closely inspected and then secured from access by anyone not authorized. Electronic devices, such as television sets, radios, lighting devices, and computers must be closely examined for explosives and electronic monitoring devices. Control is easier or more difficult depending on the location of the DV. For example, a hotel open to the public will decrease the size of the control rings, while an isolated hunting lodge or inn may allow greater protection in depth. Frequently, operating conditions are not ideal and adjustments must be made.

Finally, most assassination attempts occur while the DV is in transit. President John F. Kennedy was in an automobile when he was shot, President Reagan was entering an automobile when he was shot and there was an attempt on President Gerald Ford's life when he was moving by automobile. All of the above and more had to be incorporated into a training course for OSI agents. Once we prepared a pilot course, we could prepare and present a course of our own, without relying on other agencies. The Secret Service was very cooperative in this effort. Within a short time, OSI had trained many agents and was prepared to support the Secret Service, should the need arise. Subsequent events would make Distinguished Visitor Protection (DVP) coverage an integral part of OSI services.

One of our first DVP coverages occurred shortly after the bulletin had been written. Three of us from Special Activities were assigned to provide coverage to the Chief of Staff of the Indonesian Air Force. He would be staying at the famed Willard Hotel on Pennsylvania Avenue, a few blocks from the White House. He was to be there only a couple days. The three of us covered the hallway adjacent to his room and the elevator going up to his floor. The coverage went off without incident and we were very proud of the professional job that we had done. Just after he left, we sat in the lobby briefly, congratulating ourselves and agreeing that this was not so difficult. As we arose to depart, one of the porters stopped us and said, "Excuse me gentlemen, but did you leave this in the chair?" He produced a .30 cal. revolver that had fallen out of its holster and was left in the chair in which one of us had been sitting. Fortunately, he was aware that we were agents, thankfully he didn't know from what agency, and turned the gun over to us instead of giving it to the police. Naturally, this did not go into our report.

One of the less exciting duties that was a responsibility of the Special Activities Branch was the review of classified documents for possible downgrading. A CI organization can generate a vast volume of classified documents and as time and circumstances change, the material may be suitable for downgrading or even declassification. That is going from "Secret" to "Unclassified." Since I was the junior officer in the branch, the duty of reviewing documents fell to me. I was to read the documents and determine whether or not they could be downgraded or declassified. I discovered an astounding fact when I embarked upon this duty. Most documents are over-classified. Generating classified documents is a status thing, though unspoken and once something is classified it tends to remain so, if the decision to declassify is left to the originator. Since Special Activities generated many classified documents, the decision to downgrade or declassify went to that branch. They vehemently resisted any effort to diminish the worth of their documents. This time-consuming review gave me an intimate knowledge of past OSI operations and activities.

A friend of mine told me one day about an opening in the A&D for someone to handle PACAF, or the Pacific area. I spoke to Charles Sither, the civilian head of the A&D. He had heard about me and was interested in putting me in the PACAF section. I would be responsible for the Okinawa and Vietnam desks. I was introduced to another Charles, Charles Russell, a civilian agent who was the deputy branch chief. He also handled the Cuba desk, a duty at which he had become an expert. He had written numerous studies on Cuba and the "DGI," the Cuban intelligence organization, and studied on his own and learned to speak Spanish. Also, he had acquired a law degree and a Ph.D. His credentials were impressive and I felt that he would be a good person to work with. Time would confirm this view.

As I became familiar with my areas I discovered that not much had changed on Okinawa. The same old subversive group was agitating for return of Okinawa to Japan and removal of US bases from the island. The reports could have been written when I was there. There were the old demonstrations that attracted only a few people and articles in the Japanese language papers quoting the head of the subversives. No one seemed to be particularly excited by this threat. I knew though that we had penetrated that organization and would be instantly aware of any changes in their potential to cause mischief for the US.

Vietnam was another story. No one seemed to know exactly what was going on there. A guerrilla movement was fighting to overthrow a government headed by Ngo Dinh Diem. He was supported militarily and economically by the US. One day the future looked promising, the next events discouraged any real optimism. I knew that I would have to immerse myself in study to appreciate the problems of Vietnam and although we tended to think of the struggle as a battle between communism and democracy, we knew that Diem was ruling a country that was far from democratic. We also knew that he did not accept advice easily, especially if it suggested that he liberalize his regime. He was a Roman Catholic in a country that was overwhelmingly Buddhist. He was making every effort to suppress the Buddhist monks who were trying to get a more tolerant regime. He immediately branded them communists, which most of them were not. In the early sixties, the US supported any leader who professed to be anti-communist. Diem's

Catholicism qualified him as such a leader and the US Government embraced him.

In 1962, the US State Department conducted a three week seminar at their school located in Arlington Towers, Virginia. OSI was given one place and I asked for and was given it. The seminar consisted of lectures and films dealing with the history and government of Vietnam, including both North Vietnam and South Vietnam. Most of the speakers stressed the progress being made by Diem and emphasized the fact that the Viet Cong (VC), the guerilla movement, was a bunch of bandits and warlords who were fighting against the South Vietnamese Government for personal reasons. This position was taken by several of the US military.

Somehow, I did not feel that the problem was that simple and that there must be a political dimension to it. Based on what little study I had conducted, I knew that the VC did not just attack villages, loot them and then leave. They were destroying the whole political infrastructure of those areas in which they operated. As they killed or scared off South Vietnamese officials in the villages, they replaced them with their own. One of the speakers was Bernard Fall, an analyst who had written a book in 1961 called *Street Without Joy*, which became a classic account of the Indo-China War. His presentation criticized both the French and US approaches to the war. He compared the present situation with the struggle conducted by the Viet Minh, which led to the downfall of the French and the emergence of the Government of North Vietnam. It also resulted in the dividing of that country into two parts, one headed by Ho Chi Minh, who had defeated the French and Ngo Dinh Diem, who with US support, headed the South. Both wanted unification, on their terms, and the division could not last.

Dr. Fall had interviewed Ho Chi Minh and traveled throughout North Vietnam. His French citizenship gave him access to people and places that would be denied him were he an American citizen. He was married to an American woman and lived in the United States. He saw the problem as a political one. The North was trying to overthrow an unpopular government in the south by using guerilla warfare and subversive activities. According to Fall, any attempt to use purely conventional military tactics and strategies would be unsuccessful against a guerilla force whose goal was initially winning over the people, not just acquiring control over the land.

Despite the eloquence of his arguments, Fall was a minority of one at the seminar. The speakers, many of them State Department representatives spoke of the great progress that Diem was making in stabilizing his government and defeating the VC. Other countries in Southeast Asia, Thailand, Burma, Laos and Cambodia were covered in the seminar, but the overwhelming interest was in South Vietnam, where our commitment grew greater each day. It seemed clear that our next challenge would come from there.

When I returned from the seminar, I felt that I had a good general knowledge of the countries that I was handling. That would not be adequate enough for me to effectively review Intelligence Reports (IRs) and studies and make sound conclusions on the significance of that information. Luckily, I had only returned from the Southeast Asia Seminar a couple of months when OSI was given one place in the Strategic Intelligence School, a program offered by the US Army and taught at the Main

Navy Building on Independence Avenue. I had heard that this was one of the best schools for an intelligence neophyte to attend. It was six weeks in length and instructors were from the FBI, CIA, US Army, US Navy, and the Department of State. I was certain that it would give me knowledge of procedures for collecting, evaluating and disseminating CI material.

The school was not a disappointment. The core of the curriculum was the use of the National Intelligence Survey (NIS) prepared by CIA periodically with assistance from all the intelligence collecting agencies in the US Government. A NIS was prepared for each country of interest to the US, including friendly countries. It consisted of several sections, each dealing with a particular type of intelligence. For example, one section may deal with *Transportation*. In it would be all the intelligence available relative to the road system, rivers, railroads, airports, trucking facilities, and any other transport modes utilized in the country. An analysis of this section would give an analyst a good appreciation of how fast and efficient movement of men and supplies could be made in that country, or from that country into a neighboring one.

The NIS was the result of many analysts analyzing hundreds, perhaps thousands, of reports, each dealing with one aspect of the particular area of interest. Some of the areas of interest were relatively unchanging and needed to be examined only periodically.

For example, rivers and road capacity change slightly over a significant period of time. The size of armed forces and their disposition can change rapidly as can their capabilities and intentions.

Anyone interested in intelligence and CI analysis can

see that it is both an intellectual and an interdisciplinary function. A knowledge of economics, sociology, business and other fields of knowledge is important to the intellectual function of determining the significance of intelligence information. The relevance of many pieces of information must be determined, as well as their significance. The CI analyst, in order to understand the country and its people, must acquire the background knowledge provided by the NIS. The Strategic Intelligence School taught procedures for analyzing intelligence information. It was a valuable aid in developing an analytic capability.

The CI analyst is fortunate in that the breadth of knowledge that he needs is generally limited to intelligence concerning a country's intelligence and security organizations and perhaps its armed forces. The CI analyst usually deals in specific facts concerning the activities and capabilities of a country's intelligence organizations.

The information provided by the Strategic Intelligence School gave me the tools to acquire information, determine its relevance and significance and consolidate bits of information into a coherent report or study.

One of the speakers at the school was a Colonel Valeriano. He was active in the Filipino campaign against the Hukbalahap communist guerillas. He discussed the nature of guerrilla warfare and many techniques that could be successfully used to counter such activities. He was extremely successful in defeating the guerrillas by using innovative tactics and emphasized the fact that no anti-guerrilla movement can succeed without winning over the people. The colonel described how he used guerrilla tactics against the guerrillas and decimated their ranks. His lectures made me aware of what was necessary to defeat an incipient guerrilla movement and the kind of intelligence necessary to determine the direction of their actions. I took away the feeling that the information that I had been provided by the various lecturers would greatly assist me in developing the skills necessary for successful CI analysis.

When I returned from the school, I discovered that OSI produced studies similar to the NIS, but focused more on the intelligence and security organizations of the countries of interest. I reviewed a few that had been prepared for PACAF countries and found that the quality varied. Some studies gave a very accurate and complete description of the intelligence and security capabilities of the subject country, while others showed glaring weaknesses in that knowledge. Not surprisingly, those countries friendly to the United States were more completely reported on and the reports contained valuable information about their intelligence and security capabilities. The collection of information on so-called "friendly" countries was important for two reasons: first, we knew that they spied on us and second, we needed to know how reliable an ally they were. We needed to know their capabilities and intentions to collect intelligence against the US and what type of intelligence they were collecting. CIA was said to have discretely made the statement that, "There are no friendly foreign intelligence agencies." Whether or not CIA made that statement, it is a prudent assumption. I learned that US intelligence agencies must proceed as if it were true. This does not mean that there cannot be close collaboration between US and foreign intelligence and security agencies. Such activities must be carried out with the greatest of caution. One of the greatest dangers that espionage by friendly countries presents is the possibility that although they may not use it against us, the fact is that we have lost control over sensitive information that might fall into the hands of a country who would use it against us.

Another thing the school taught me was the importance of "Biographic Information." This is particularly important when dealing with other intelligence agencies, but it is also important in connection with high ranking military and civilian leaders. This is an area often neglected in collection activities. Knowing whether a member of a friendly intelligence or security organization can speak several languages, has lived or trained in the United States, has expressed pro or anti-American sympathies are all important pieces of information that can help the person dealing with that individual. I remembered that our biographic collection on Okinawa was found wanting and had it been more comprehensive, support from police and other Okinawan officials might have been greatly enhanced. I remembered also that we received few biographic reports from other agencies. It was a fruitful area of collection that was neglected.

When I returned to the Directorate to assume my analysis duties I was eager to use the training that the Strategic Intelligence School had given me. Although I had written many CI reports during my tour on Okinawa, I submitted them in draft form to the District Office. There they were finalized and their importance and reliability were commented upon in a finished IR. I was also aware that those units in the field were engaged in what might be called the "numbers racket." That is, they attempted to publish as many IRs as possible without much attention being paid to the quality of the information. One example, I am sorry to say, came from a report published on Okinawa. A meeting was held at which five known subversives attended. Five reports were written to recognize this fact. I immediately prepared a letter for the A&D Branch Manager's signature which stated that one report, with cross-referencing could more properly report such information instead of five reports, each duplicating the other.

Field units were also cautioned to stop a procedure which could lead to compromise of sources. Some reports that listed people at a meeting left out the name of the source who attended the meeting and reported the information to OSI. If the report were ever compromised the omission of that name could point to the identity of the OSI source. Each IR identified the nature of the subject matter, e.g. *Espionage Activity*. The report also contained an evaluation of the information in the report. A number and a letter was used to evaluate both the source and the information. For example an A-1 report said that the source was reliable (A) and that the information was correct (I). Conversely, an F-6 report indicated that the reliability of the source could not be determined and that the truthfulness of the information was unknown. The selection of these categories was, at best, a subjective evaluation by the author of the report and it appeared that little thought was actually given to these evaluations.

The evaluation system did create a problem. OSI personnel who were untrained in analysis developed a philosophy that recognized that reports not marked with a high reliance on the source and a high probability of truthfulness of the information were somehow denigrating the collection activity of the collection office. As a result of this misunderstanding of the evaluation system, a few District Offices would not allow any reports released unless they contained a reliable rating for both the source and the information. This practice was totally unprofessional and had to be stopped. Later, when in Vietnam, I was ordered by my superior not to submit any reports that did not reflect a reliable source and accurate information. I stated that such an order must be in writing and that I would contact the Directorate and ask for a ruling on that order. The person backed down, and after some discussion, acknowledged that perhaps he was wrong.

Few people in OSI were really interested in analysis work and, lacking this interest, considered such effort less important than counterespionage operations. It was difficult to staff headquarters and field positions with people who were knowledgeable and motivated. I later discovered that same problem plagued both the CIA and the FBI, although neither would be eager to admit it. Collection and operational activities have always been given the most publicity because of the, not incorrect, belief that they are exciting and demanding. Analysis, on the other hand, lacks the dynamism that those activities supposedly entail. It is a truism, that unless the information collected is properly collated, analyzed and disseminated, it is valueless. Years later, we would set up a two week analysis course for agents from the field. This not only improved the image of analysis, but gave those agents a greater respect for the importance of their work.

The Special Reports that were periodically written were challenging and added to the knowledge of the area being reported. If an analyst spent several weeks researching all reports and studies related to a specific country, he invariably became somewhat of an authority on that country. Based on the FBI influence, it was the practice of OSI to use an unattractive blue cover. All special reports sported this same colored cover. A friend of mine, who worked at the Pentagon, remarked to me one day that he didn't know whether or not he had received a certain special report. His comment was that, "They all looked the same." At first I was irritated by his comment; but then I realized that we were producing an important product and why should it not be packaged attractively? After some thought, I went to Charlie Sither (who incidentally was an ex-FBI agent) and asked that we consider using a different colored cover for each special report. I delicately pointed out that there was nothing wrong for the FBI to use the same cover over and over, but we should show more innovation and make our product eye-catching.

With considerable support from Charlie Russell, I convinced Charlie Sither that we should at least try to break out of the rut we were in. Charlie Sither was an outstanding manager who welcomed new ideas, even those that were unproven. I had more trouble convincing May Ideta, the civilian analyst who managed our publications. Her outstanding education and writing skill greatly added to our publications acceptability. She was somewhat conservative and felt that we did not need to "jazz up" our publications. I somehow convinced her that we should at least try to make our reports more attractive. Having gotten May Ideta's reluctant approval, I went to Charlie Sither and suggested that we begin our new cover with the next special report. It turned out to be one that my section was completing. I do not remember the country that was the subject of the report, but I went down to the OSI printing shop and spoke with the sergeant who was in charge.

Master Sergeant Smith, naturally called "Smitty" by everyone, was very blunt and not reluctant to express an opinion. He had wondered why we had continued to use that same "grubby" blue cover over the years. He agreed that it did not add to the attractiveness of the reports. I asked what colors, other than blue, he had available. Smitty advised that the question, more importantly, was how much card stock did he have? He needed hundreds of covers for our reports which used two covers, front and back. He normally used only blue and didn't know what he had on hand in sufficient quantities to provide covers for the hundreds of copies that one report entailed. Perhaps foolishly, I told him to use colored card stock that he had sufficient quantities of, other than blue. He promised me that he would "take care of it."

The following week, May Ideta called me and said that the printing, using a different colored cover was ready and was being brought up from the print shop by Sergeant Smith himself. I hurried down to May's office and arrived at the same time as Master Sergeant Smith. Both May and I looked at the cart which contained the reports. The covers were a very bright canary yellow. Even I was shocked, as was May, who, remember was somewhat conservative. Neither of us said anything until May finally suggested that I be the one to let Charlie Sither see the first "non-blue" cover. As I left for his office, May, without comment, accompanied me. I stuck my head in the door to see if he was busy and Charlie Sither motioned me in. I saw that Charlie Russell was there also. Unconsciously, I had carried the copy of the new cover behind me. I placed it in front of them and waited for a reaction. There was not any discernible reaction from the two Charlies until Charlie Sither said, "You know, it's not bad once you get used to it." From then on, every section used a different colored cover for their reports. I must admit that no one ever used that same canary yellow, but there were a variety of colors that clearly differentiated the reports. As I look back on it, I hope that OSI is still using different colors for their reports and that the FBI has gotten away from that "grubby" blue.

Reports from Vietnam continued to paint a rosy picture relative to the progress in the war. Reports from the State Department especially presented a picture of a war that we had almost won. Equally optimistic were reports from our Military Assistance Advisory Group (MAAG). American media sources were not always in agreement with the optimistic assessment. They were mostly ignored by the government which did not give much weight to opinions of non-military observers. The press reports reminded me of the seminar that I had attended and of what Bernard Fall had said about the political nature of the guerrilla movement. At the same time, Madame Nhu, the wife of President Diem's brother, Ngo Dinh Nhu was traveling the United States and being highly critical of US efforts to assist South Vietnam and demanding greater support for the South Vietnamese Government.

At the same time that there were demands from the military and the State Department for further US involvement, the crisis of the Buddhist monks heated up. As they asked for greater representation and reforms, Diem used brutal tactics to suppress their complaints.

Pagodas were raided by South Vietnamese troops and many of the bonzes (priests) were arrested. On May 8, 1963, Buddhists had gathered in the northern city of Hue to celebrate the birthday of Buddha, police attacked the gathering and killed nine people. In June, 1963, a Buddhist monk, Thich Quang Duc burned himself in downtown Saigon, the nation's capital. This was photographed by a US reporter. The picture of the burning monk appeared throughout world newspapers. This brought about a very dramatic and shocking move from the Buddhists. A few of them sat down in a main street and had themselves doused with gasoline. They then set fire to themselves. Photographs of these self-immolations appeared in the world press again, and, at least outside of the US, public opinion was very critical of Diem. Many people in the US began to wonder about the Diem regime. Americans did not appreciate Madam Nhu's joking reference to "bonze fires" and "barbeques."

An event that was very symbolic of the situation faced by the United States occurred in early January, 1963. Forty miles southeast of Saigon, the village of Ap Bac was the scene of a battle staged by the Army of Vietnam (ARVN). Aware of the forthcoming attack, the Communist Main Force Battalion entrenched themselves and set up strong defensive positions. Consisting of about 350 men, the VC wreaked havoc among the attacking ARVN troops. At a loss of only eighteen men killed and about forty wounded, the VC killed eighty ARVN troops and wounded over 100. As a result of the action, five US helicopters were shot down. The ARVN displayed a lack of fire discipline, were confused, and refused to advance into the VC fire. The VC unquestionably outfought the ARVN troops and rapidly disengaged and escaped.

Remarkably, the US Army tried to put a spin on the event by claiming that Ap Bac had been secured and thus the engagement was successful. There was no mention of the fact that it was secured after the disengagement by the VC and that ARVN paratroopers had to be dropped into the battle to save the situation. The significance of the event was the fact that ARVN troops who outnumbered the VC, were transported by US helicopters and received US assistance in the planning of the operation displayed cowardice and confusion and were outfought by the VC. Several US newsmen witnessed the battle and reported also that there was no support for the operation from higher level ARVN Commanders. This began the media's disenchantment with the Government of Vietnam (GVN) and their coverage of events became more and more critical of that government and the US support.

As an analyst, I seriously questioned the chance for success of the US support for Diem's government. But, I had not been to Vietnam yet and reports from those who were there downplayed the fiasco at Ap Bac and relegated its position to yesterday's news. The optimism from the US Army continued; as it did from Secretary of Defense McNamara, who announced that he saw the "light at the end of the tunnel." I continued to try and support the "party line," seeking to objectively evaluate the situation while respecting the views of people senior and more experienced than I, people who had been to Vietnam and were ostensibly speaking with authority.

At the time things seemed to be disintegrating in South Vietnam, Charlie Sither was promoted out of the A&D and was replaced by a Lieutenant Colonel. The replacement was cautious to a fault. Anytime I wrote anything critical of the US effort in Vietnam, I was called up and asked to justify that position and when I did, the writing was severely toned down. It was an open secret in the intelligence community that the VC were using Cambodia to send additional troops down into South Vietnam. Cambodia was part of what later came to be called the "Ho Chi Minh Trail" I had referred to this fact in a study that I prepared. He insisted on changing my comment to, "The VC may be using Cambodia," rather than "were."

Suddenly, there was a complete change in the nature of reports coming from the intelligence community. There were very few criticisms directed at the US effort in South Vietnam. Reporting was almost void of any objective evaluation of the effort. Instead, many reports merely quoted the Administration's public utterances. We discussed this phenomenon and jokingly referred to it as the "light at the end of the tunnel syndrome."

Something else occurred which probably should not have been surprising. There was, amongst the military, certainly the Air Force and the Army, the view that going to Vietnam was the best way to "get one's ticket punched." In other words, those going there would assure their promotions. The press reported the fact that many Army officers referred to Vietnam as "The Laboratory." Many sought assignments to Vietnam "before the opportunities ended." This attitude did not reach OSI and no one was making a supreme effort to go there. In fact, we had sent a few agents into Vietnam and they had great difficulty in getting cooperation from either the Vietnamese or the US Army. Once again inter-service rivalry and parochial politics was hampering the overall mission. Reporting from Vietnam by OSI was very sparse. Word came down to us that the US Army, in the form of the Military Assistance Command Vietnam (MACV) was "in charge and looming large." There was to be a competition between the Air Force and the Army as to who actually ran things in Vietnam. MACV was in the driver's seat and intended to remain there. The USAF was fighting this ascendancy by increasing its personnel in Vietnam and providing more advisory services to the Vietnamese Air Force (VNAF). As Air Force units were assigned to various bases in Vietnam, the need for CI support increased. The US Army Intelligence was not usually present on airbases and could not be counted on for that support. There was practically no cooperation between USAF intelligence organizations, including OSI, and Army Military Intelligence. By this time, the CIC had been absorbed into the Army's Military Intelligence.

The OSI mission was going to be greatly expanded by events in South Vietnam, particularly as the Air Force presence increased markedly. Charlie Russell and I were called in by the Chief, Counterintelligence Division and given the assignment of determining the nature of the role to be played by OSI in its CI mission, in an unconventional warfare situation. We were to set up guidelines for operations and put them in a concrete form. Fortunately, Charlie was extremely well informed about guerrillas and unconventional warfare. He had studied the history of guerrilla warfare and was literally an expert on Castro's successful war against the dictator Fulgencio Batista. As Assistant Branch Chief, he had read all of the reports and studies emanating from OSI's A&D Branch. He and I had discussed the problem frequently and were in agreement as to how to proceed.

We decided that the mission to provide CI support had not changed at all. OSI was charged with protecting the USAF against sabotage, espionage, and subversion. What had changed was the environment in which we were now planning to operate. The physical protection of USAF bases was ordinarily in the hands of the US Army. At that time, the US Army had no combat units in South Vietnam and the Air Force Security Police were not trained in defensive infantry operations. It was our conclusion that OSI was limited by the fact that areas surrounding the airbases were in hostile control and that venturing out beyond the limits of those airbases was not feasible. Lacking the capability to protect its agents the OSI had to conduct its operations on the bases. While this approach failed to provide adequate CI cover beyond base perimeters it was all that OSI could do under the limited capabilities present at that time. We were very much aware of the limiting effect of such a philosophy; but it appeared to be satisfactory for the moment. This examination prompted us to decide that if the USAF wanted security for its bases, it would have to provide it. Coincidentally, while we were discussing the matter, the Security Police were in the process of planning a whole new concept of operations for their people. Ultimately, they were to be trained in combat defensive tactics including perimeter security and the employment of heavy firepower (e.g. mortars and heavy machine guns).

The Air Force set up a short Counterinsurgency Course that was to be taught at the Air University at Montgomery, Alabama. Charlie Russell and I were invited down to lecture on "Counterintelligence Against Guerrillas." We received such a favorable response that we were asked to give the same lecture to the class at the

Air War College. When we lectured to the Air War College, which was composed of high ranking officers, the subject of Vietnam came up frequently and we were asked to give our evaluation of the situation. Ignoring the "party line" we pointed out the many distressing aspects of that conflict and our inability to get President Diem to institute needed reforms. Several people asked if the use of American troops would be necessary. At the time, there were about 7000 US armed forces members in Southeast Asia.

I remembered that our reply was that while some US forces might help, the real question was how to win over the people of South Vietnam. We did not think that the increased presence of American troops would help the South Vietnamese Government in its goal of winning over the people it had disaffected. We did allow that because of the deteriorating military situation, it might be necessary to bring in American combat troops to prevent a complete takeover by the VC and its sponsor, North Vietnam. While we did not feel that a takeover was imminent, it could be an ultimate possibility.

One officer pointed out that our evaluation seemed to contradict the statements that the government was making about our progress in Vietnam. Our response was that our evaluation was based on the intelligence we had received and analyzed and our only purpose was to present the situation as we saw it. Many of those present acknowledged the fact that many of the news media had offered similar opinions. It was around this point in time (early 1963) that there developed a definite rupture in relations between the Administration and the media. The word from the top was that the media was critical of US efforts to the point where they were aiding the enemy. It is true that after the Ap Bac debacle the media adopted a dubious attitude toward military pronouncements.

The situation between the military and the media became a serious problem, which the Administration probably underestimated. The media had access to the American public and their reporting reached millions of Americans. Their view was that if it was news it should be reported. This did not set well with the military who felt that some things detracted from support for the war effort and gave heart to the VC.

Reports that contradicted and often embarrassed the Administration appeared frequently and some reporters would not accept anything given out at press briefings. OSI received a clipping service which covered almost every major newspaper and news magazine in the United States. We started monitoring those articles dealing with Vietnam and found a striking departure from what the official government positions were. There were frequent disagreements between the military and the media in matters dealing with the progress of the war, the number of VC still active and the number of VC killed.

We conducted a review of past progress reports and estimates of VC numbers and casualties. There did not seem to be any consistency in the figures. No matter what kind of reverse had taken place, the progress was always great and it was impossible to determine actual VC losses and present strengths. MACV figures for enemy killed were always higher than those offered by the CIA. The optimism expressed by the military was often not shared by the CIA. At that time, CIA had a large presence in Vietnam, both at Saigon and out in the field. They had people in places where the military did not.

We had a small group of agents in South Vietnam in

1962. None of them had any experience in Southeast Asia and they had no Vietnamese language capability. It is extremely risky for a CI organization to rely on non-American interpreters. OSI did it then and throughout the war. Some language capability was developed but it was extremely limited. This problem existed throughout the US intelligence community. When CIA opened its office in Berlin, at the beginning of the Cold War they did not have a Russian linguist case officer. (Note: CIA calls their operating people case officers and OSI calls theirs' agents.)

There were reasons why we lacked this language capability. First, most volunteers preferred to attend language courses in German, French, and Spanish. Few were interested in studying what the language experts called "exotic" languages. Languages like Arabic, Russian, Chinese and Japanese were not highly desirable because of their difficulty. Not surprisingly, OSI was way over on German, French and Spanish linguists. Years later, just before I left OSI, I conducted a survey for the Director of OSI on OSI utilization of language trained agents. I found that 68% (this was in 1979) of language trained agents were not assigned to countries in which they were language trained. There were examples of agents trained in Greek being sent to Alaska and Italian trained agents going to the UK. Lack of foreign language skills has been a major problem for US Intelligence and CI since before World War II and OSI fared no better than other agencies in dealing with it. Today, when we must face a worldwide terrorist threat, we hear many people state that we must develop language capability in Middle Eastern languages. This need for language capability was learned in Vietnam and somehow forgotten.

Something else, the US intelligence community learned in Vietnam was the need for people who possessed a good knowledge of the cultures of other countries. Few Americans knew anything about Vietnam when we became involved. As the war continued, many people in the intelligence and CI fields tried to acquire knowledge of that country's customs and cultures in order to enhance their capabilities. OSI tried to provide background information to its agents assigned there, but no formalized briefing program was ever set up.

Today, we are involved with the threat of worldwide terrorism emanating from the Middle East. The languages involved, principally Arabic and Farsi, are almost unknown in the US, except by people who have come to the US from that area. Now we are talking about recruiting people who speak those languages and training others to speak them. The training of a person to speak any language is time consuming and effectiveness in the language does not come quickly. The training of linguists should be a number one priority in the US Government in general and in intelligence in particular. During my OSI career, the lack of sufficient foreign language capability was always a serious problem that went largely unnoticed, not only by OSI, but by the whole intelligence community.

When I arrived at OSI Headquarters, I found out that liaison was more of a social thing than a business function. Agencies exchanged liaison officers who periodically visited and supposedly received information from them. The truth is there was a climate of suspicion, unspoken, but nevertheless there, which prevented any real exchanges.

During my tour at OSI Headquarters, I was never

aware of our receiving any really worthwhile information from either the FBI or the CIA. We did receive reports from those agencies; but they would probably have been sent to us whether or not we had a liaison officer. None of the reports were of any great value and provided, at best, background information.

There seemed to be a belief that any information given to another agency was sure to be compromised. We had the "Third Agency Rule" which prohibited us from giving any reports that we received from the FBI to another US agency. This restriction was supposedly to avoid false confirmation of information. While that may be one reason to limit the information it did inhibit any real exchange of information between agencies who received FBI reports. The few reports that the CIA gave us were usually of better quality than those of the FBI, but they never supplied anything that was really not available from other sources. I found reports from allies, particularly those dealing with the Far East, to be informative and well written. Unfortunately, these reports were few in number and dealt with specific issues rather than general CI situations.

WELCOME TO VIETNAM

By the spring of 1963, OSI was getting more involved in the CI effort in South Vietnam. I found out that the position of Chief, Counterintelligence, would be open in summer of that year. I volunteered for it and was given the assignment. I would be responsible for managing the CI Division in the Vietnam District Office. I was eager to see if I could improve the situation and also to try out the operating philosophy that we had established.

In July of 1963 I boarded a plane for South Vietnam. Before we departed from Travis Air Force Base, California, I discovered that another OSI agent was on the plane with me. Special Agent Bill Griffies was going over to become the Chief, Criminal Investigations Division. He had been the Detachment Commander at Houston, Texas. During his tour there he had attended night school and completed his Law Degree. He had not been given the chance to take the bar examination and would have to take it when he completed his one year tour in South Vietnam. I was impressed with his knowledge of CI as well as his skill in the criminal investigations area. I felt that we would work well together and found out later that this was true.

After a long and tiring flight, we arrived at Tan Son Nhut Airport near Saigon, South Vietnam. While we were waiting for transportation, we saw three Air Force trucks proceeding slowly toward a USAF transport parked near the terminal. Each truck contained a coffin draped with the US flag. Suddenly, all conversation ceased and we each held our private thoughts as we waited to be taken to the OSI District Office.

It was midday when we arrived in Vietnam and it took no time to reach the OSI Office, which was located at Tan Son Nhut airbase, where the civil traffic also landed. We were immediately introduced to the District Commander, a Lieutenant Colonel Sharpe. He welcomed us to Vietnam and gave us a quick briefing about the situation. It seemed that any CI work that we attempted to do off-base was coordinated with the Vietnamese Military Security Service (MSS). Criminal investigations requiring off-base efforts would be coordinated with the Vietnamese police. Seeing that we were tired, Sharpe released us to be taken to downtown Saigon to a hotel, which would be temporary quarters for us.

The hotel where we were to stay was named the "Majestic." It had definitely seen better days, and in no way could it be considered "majestic." Every part of it was old and rundown. It was, however, air conditioned, which made up for its wretched condition. We were told by the sergeant who accompanied us that the South Vietnamese had broken up a cell of VC at the Majestic only two weeks ago. Seven men were detained for questioning. According to the sergeant, "detained for questioning" meant that no one would see any of these persons again. Such measures were reminiscent of what took place in Nazi Germany. But then, drastic circumstances may have required drastic measures.

Bill Griffies and I were to share a large room at the Majestic, until we could locate private quarters. All of the OSI agents lived in private quarters, while our non-agent enlisted personnel lived in tents on Tan Son Nhut airbase. Bill and I immediately started asking questions about private rentals in Saigon. We found out that there were many rentals available, some in apartment buildings owned by Frenchmen. We first got settled in to our room and then started to look for someplace to eat. Prior to leaving our room, we set "search traps," which involved arranging some things in a certain way so that it could be easily determined if someone had disturbed them. We placed a rubber band around a small jewelry box and measured its distance from the end of the box precisely. When we returned, we found that the box had been disturbed; the rubber band was nowhere near the spot we had placed it.

Agent Jene Hunter took us to lunch at a French restaurant named Brodard's. It was located on Tu Do Street, the main street of Saigon; a beautiful tree lined street that stretched from the Saigon River to the Catholic Cathedral on John F. Kennedy Circle, a distance of about ten blocks. The Majestic was at the end of Tu Do Street that intersected the river. There were shops and restaurants all along Tu Do Street and only two or three bars, which catered to the few Americans and Frenchmen living in Saigon.

The numerous tailor shops had signs which proclaimed that a suit could be made for you in only a few days. These tailors were mostly Indians and seemed to have a corner on the tailoring market in Saigon. I would discover later that they also were involved in the black market money exchanges throughout Saigon.

Special Agent Jene Hunter was a graduate of Vietnamese language school, a twelve month course. He said that he could understand much of what was said, but had great difficulty in making the Vietnamese understand him. He had been ill and placed on light duty. He was forced to spend a portion of each day sunning himself at the swimming pool of the Circle Sportif, a private, high class French club frequented by rich Frenchmen, Vietnamese and the US Ambassador. Jene had specifically been sent to Vietnam to help set up what would be known as the Saigon Interrogation Center. This was to be a joint facility staffed by the South Vietnamese, the CIA and US Military Intelligence and CI personnel. He was very enthusiastic about his mission and approached it in a professional manner. Unfortunately, the Center was never set up during the time that he was there, due primarily to the fact that there could never be any accord on how to proceed. He turned out to be very helpful to the CI Division.

Bill Griffies and I found an apartment on Tu Do Street that was offered by a Frenchman. He was openly disdainful of Americans and overcharged us, as did all the landlords in Saigon. The apartment was just across the street from the newly built Caravelle Hotel, which was the closest thing there that resembled a moderately modern American hotel. Its prices were the highest in Saigon and it was populated by US newsmen and airline personnel. It was said that they did a lot of their reporting from there. It had a restaurant which had telephones on each table. One could call any other table. This must have been a French idea, because it did not last long; the phones were removed after a couple of weeks. It did have evening floor shows which normally consisted of French entertainers, whom I reluctantly admitted were some-times quite talented.

One of the shows was put on by a young Frenchman who had traveled from Europe to Southeast Asia on a motorcycle. I wondered how he was able to safely cross areas controlled by the VC. I would find out later that the

French played both sides and tried to benefit from the situation. In any case, this fellow had a good singing voice and was very entertaining. Many of the businesses, especially restaurants, were owned by Frenchmen. None of these French associated with Americans. In fact, they displayed a rudeness that was unmistakably directed at Americans. The Vietnamese, for reasons I could not understand, treated them as though they were royalty.

An example of just how rude they could be was demonstrated when Bill Griffies and I were having lunch in a floating restaurant on the Saigon River. We had just been seated when two Frenchmen came in shortly after us. One of the Frenchmen screamed at the Vietnamese in rapid French. Bill Griffies, without saying a word, left our table and walked over to the two Frenchmen. He addressed the one who had done the screaming in English, Bill asked him if he understood English. He cautiously advised that he did. Then Bill told him that if he opened his mouth again and said anything critical of Americans, he would toss him into the river. Bill showed a determination that made the Frenchman cower. He then walked back to our table and said that the Frenchman had bullied the waiter because he had waited on us first. Bill also added that he was from Louisiana and that French was a second language to him. Vive la France!

The French influence was strong in Saigon. Vietnamese who could afford it, sent their children to French schools, ate at French restaurants, and dressed like the French. In fact, Tu Do Street was known to every taxi and cyclo driver as Rue Catinat. The style of cooking in most of the best restaurants was French. One could walk down Tu Do Street almost anytime and smell the hypnotizing odor of French onion soup.

When we started working, we made the discovery that the Vietnamese observed what we called a "siesta." Every workday between 12:30 P.M. and 03:30 P.M. everyone stopped what they were doing and rested. OSI did not adopt that custom, and so we found that when we visited any of our Vietnamese counterparts we had to see them before noon or after three. We had been out in the Saigon heat and were thoroughly disheveled while our counterparts were freshly bathed and wearing fresh clothes. I really regretted the fact that we could not adapt to circumstances. What we ended up doing was to make our calls after 03:30 P.M. and then go home, shower and prepare for dinner. We were adaptable.

The first official meeting I had was with a Major Trong who was the MSS Operations Officer for the Saigon area. He spoke English very well and was extremely cordial. I told him what our mission was and asked how we could be of any assistance to the MSS. He said that they needed automobiles for their work and asked if we could provide any to them. After I recovered from the shock I told him that I would look into it. I found out later that he had been dealing with the CIA and that things like air conditioners and Rolex watches (he was wearing a gold Rolex) were regular items designed to facilitate liaison with the MSS.

There was no way that OSI could match CIA contributions. I realized that the carton of cigarettes or the occasional bottle of whiskey that were welcomed on Okinawa would do us no good there. I did find Major Trong very receptive to my request that we meet periodically to discuss matters of mutual interest. He asked me how I felt about the problems that the South Vietnamese Government was having with the Buddhists. I told him that I had only been in country a few days and did not know much about the internal problems. He smiled as if he appreciated my tactful answer. He was not satisfied with the answer and followed it with a question about whether or not I thought a coup might take place against President Diem. I thought that I would try a little honesty and responded that there was certainly a chance of a coup if the people were as disaffected as the American press indicated. He asked me what the Americans would do if a coup took place. I said that I could not speak for the US but I thought that the Vietnamese people should be able to elect their own government and oust any government that they found unsuitable. Realizing that I had taken a greater step than I had planned, I offered no other comments.

Major Trong, I realized was feeling me out to see if I would reveal to him how the US would feel about a coup against Diem. We agreed to meet again for lunch the following week. He wanted to introduce me to a golf course near Saigon that had a remarkable restaurant. Then he surprised me by saying that we could talk more frankly there. He obviously felt that his office was insecure. I left him with the feeling that he sincerely wanted to cooperate with us, but had limitations placed on him which did not allow full cooperation. Then I suddenly wondered if I had misspoken. I did not know where he stood relative to a coup against Diem; but I felt that he was not trying to entrap me, but was interested from the standpoint of someone who was possibly involved in planning a coup.

I left Major Trong's office feeling that I had hit it off well with him. I mentioned that I was looking forward to lunch the following week. When I returned to my office,

I talked to Colonel Sharpe who was rather plain spoken. He asked how I liked Major Trong. I said that I was very impressed with him and thought he might be a good contact. He then asked if I knew Trong's religion. I said no that I had not gotten to know him that well yet. Sharpe then advised me that Trong was a devout Buddhist. The colonel had read an IR, from another US agency, that confirmed Trong's religious affiliation. I did not describe my conversation with Trong to Colonel Sharpe because I had not been certain of its import.

I suddenly realized the significance of my conversation with Trong. As a devout Buddhist he could not approve of the terror tactics that Diem was using against them. I believed that he was attempting to find out my and OSI's feeling about a coup.

I knew I could be wrong, but I looked forward to my coming luncheon to see what he had in mind. Later, I spoke with Jene Hunter who told me that he respected Trong and that he thought Trong had been cooperative. In his personal opinion, Trong was anti-Diem. Jene added that other Vietnamese officers that he met were openly critical of Diem when talking to Americans. I asked Jene if there was a coup attempt, did he think Major Trong would be involved in it. He said that as Operations Officer for the Saigon Region, Trong would have to be won over. He was in a position to compromise any planning that might be going on, if he was not included in the coup effort.

The following week, I met Major Trong at the golf course outside of Saigon. I was nervous about going there alone and carried the small Browning .25 cal. semi-automatic pistol I had purchased before I left the United States. I arrived at the golf course and proceeded to the restaurant. I was more at ease when I realized that it was a very public place. There were French, Americans and Vietnamese there. Major Trong was seated at a table and beckoned me over. He was wearing civilian clothes. We had a lobster salad, which was outstanding. I waited for him to tell me the purpose of this meeting. No one was seated near us, but he talked in a low voice. We finished our lunch and then he asked me if I knew about the crisis in Vietnam. I replied that it had been given worldwide press coverage. He smiled and said don't you know any more than that. I decided to be frank with him and told him that it appeared to me that a coup attempt was likely.

Major Trong stated that he knew that the Americans had lost patience with Diem and would welcome a change in government. I did not comment. Then he said that there was a coup coming that was to be carried out by "patriotic" Vietnamese. The coup would take place within a couple of months and those involved hoped to receive support from the Americans. He implied that support from the US in the form of encouragement had already been obtained. I then asked him why he would tell me such sensitive information. He said that he wanted the Americans to be aware of the upcoming action for their own safety. The coup would not change the relationship that Vietnam had with the US. The coup leaders would be people that no one would expect to go against Diem. He then mentioned General Duong Van Minh (called Big Minh because of his stature) and a couple of other Generals that I was not familiar with.

He concluded that he could not tell me the exact date and time, but that prior to the coup, the Vietnamese Marines would be moved to the zoological garden in Saigon. He then excused himself and departed. I immediately returned to my office and briefed Colonel Sharpe. He called in one of the enlisted agents who worked for me and gave him the information and asked him to comment on it. The agent smiled and said that the information was ridiculous. First, he said, General Minh was a staunch supporter of Diem and would not take part in any coup. I knew that he had been collecting information for the last nine months and I respected his experience, if not his arrogance. I directed him to coordinate with the US Army Intelligence the next day.

The next day when he returned from Saigon I expected him to report to me and brief me on what he had found out. Instead, he went directly into the colonel's office.

I waited until he came out and asked him to come in and see me. I queried him about the information that I had given him to evaluate. He repeated what he had said the previous day, that such a coup was very unlikely. He said that the US Army Intelligence had been particularly negative concerning the possibility of a coup occurring, as the report described.

The next day, I prepared an IR which stated essentially what Trong had told me. I added at the end of my report that, "Reliable US intelligence agencies have advised that such a coup is extremely unlikely; and that General Minh is loyal to President Diem and would not take part in any revolt against him." I thought to myself, as the report was sent out, that it was of little value because it was repetitive of other knowledgeable US sources. As days passed, I remembered Trong's comment about moving the Vietnamese Marines to the zoological gardens just before the coup. I drove by there a few times during the ensuing weeks and saw no sign of the Marines. On October 30, 1963 I drove by the gardens and observed Vietnamese Marines setting up camp. It appeared that they were in the process of moving in. I recognized them by their distinctive camouflage fatigues which were different from the ordinary Army fatigues.

I reported back to Colonel Sharpe the fact that part of the information about the coup had been confirmed. His response was that the Vietnamese constantly moved their forces around Saigon and that it probably did not indicate that anything was going to happen. By then I was convinced that, for whatever reason, Major Trong had given me false information. Perhaps he wanted to see what I would do with it, or maybe he wanted to mislead us as to when the planned coup was really about to take place. The presence of the Marines in the zoological garden was the one piece of information that argued for the report's authenticity.

The next morning, at about 07:30 A.M., Bill Griffies and I left our apartment and proceeded down Tu Do Street. Suddenly, we heard the sound of cannon fire. As we crossed one of the streets which intersected Tu Do, we saw a Vietnamese tank firing into the Vietnamese Special Forces barracks. We knew that the Special Forces were controlled by Ngo Dinh Nhu, Diem's brother and counselor. We drove past the street and continued, without incident, to Tan Son Nut airbase. When we arrived we could hear small arms fire all around the base, though it did not appear that there was any firing directed at the base.

The only person at our office was an administrative airman. He immediately approached us and advised that he was burning trash near the base perimeter and heard a lot of firing. He thought that the fire was directed at him and hurried back to our office. We assured him that he was not the object of all the firing that was going on around us.

I went to the USAF Headquarters and asked to see General Rollen Anthis, the USAF Commander in South Vietnam. I was directed by an airman to the rear of the General's office. He and some of his staff were looking down on the Saigon River and observing the Vietnamese Navy firing at Vietnamese planes that appeared to be attacking the ships. The fire from the ships did not even come close to the aircraft as they dove down on the ships. One of those present said, "Look at those guys fly; we trained them." Someone else present said, "Yeah, we trained those Navy gunners too." An officer arrived and was getting into a flak jacket. The General was not in a good mood and asked the officer, why in hell he was putting the jacket on. I told the General that we were going back into town to see just what was going on. The General acknowledged that that was a good idea and we departed for Saigon.

We drove back into Saigon with firing going on all around us. No one stopped us or offered any resistance to our journey. We arrived back at our apartment and waited for some sign of what was actually happening. Jene Hunter arrived, in uniform, and armed. He had observed tanks being moved around the city and troops also being placed in certain spots. He said that no one bothered him or attempted to stop him. Bill Griffies and I decided that we felt safer in civilian clothes. We had brought AR15s, a rifle which was the predecessor of the M16. The Air Force had purchased several thousand after General Le May, the Chief of the Strategic Air Command (SAC), saw a demonstration and was greatly impressed by the gun. It held twenty rounds of ammunition and could fire fully automatic, making it an effective submachine gun. We waited all afternoon before we ventured out again, as there was quite a bit of gunfire coming from the streets around us.

As night drew near, the firing seemed to subside considerably. We decided that going out into the street after dark was not a good idea and settled in for the night. We discussed the situation and decided that anyone who tried to enter the apartment complex would be fired upon. We did not know to what extent the VC might try to take advantage of the situation and launch attacks against both the South Vietnamese and the Americans. At about ten o'clock, the streets went almost silent, with only an occasional shot being fired. None of the firing appeared to be close to our apartment area or downtown Saigon. Apparently, the VC were also caught asleep.

After a somewhat sleepless night we all decided to try and make our way back to Tan Son Nhut airbase. There was no sound of firing. The streets looked deserted, as they generally did at 07:00 A.M. As we proceeded toward Tan Son Nhut we suddenly saw military trucks and cars that were riddled with bullets. As we proceeded further we saw Vietnamese Military Police, with the big white "QC" on their helmets. They waved us on and made no effort to stop us. We arrived at Tan Son Nhut without incident. When we arrived at the OSI Office, some of our enlisted agents, who lived in another part of Saigon, had also made it to the base without incident. We found out that our non-agent enlisted personnel had spent the night in their tents, unarmed and wondering what was going to happen to them.

The coup was over and we did not know who was in

charge of South Vietnam. General Anthis advised that he had heard from the State Department that indeed a coup had occurred and that General Duong Van Minh (Big Minh) was now in charge. Later that afternoon, we found out from some of our American Embassy contacts that Diem and his brother Nhu had both been assassinated by soldiers during the coup. They had hidden in a tunnel that ran from the Catholic church on John F. Kennedy Circle to the Presidential Palace. Within a few days we saw a photograph of their bodies in an armored personnel carrier. Nhu's body had numerous stab wounds in it. The tyrannical reign was over and we now had to try and establish contact with our new Vietnamese counterparts.

Gradually, we found out who had taken over and were made aware of the fact that all the plotters were still jockeying for position and the government was by no means solidified under an accepted slate of leaders. During the next few months there would be seven coups and changes in government. It was impossible to establish any relationships with the people moving into the higher echelons of intelligence. They changed frequently. Our CI efforts were confined to trying to get information from the CIA, who, if they were honest, would have admitted that they were as confused and cut off as we were. Remarkably, the VC did not take advantage of the military upheaval and conduct guerrilla activities. There were absolutely no reports of any VC activity either during or immediately after the coup. An acquaintance from the American Embassy, who would not admit it, but was definitely CIA, advised that he thought that the VC took advantage of the coup to move men and supplies into their safe havens located in and around the Saigon area.

Prior to and shortly after the coup, the VC made it a practice to plant package bombs in areas where Americans might congregate. There was a restaurant which was unofficially named, "The Birdwatchers." It was located on a corner on Tu Do street and was open on two sides. One day, about 12:00 A.M., when it was fairly crowded, a bomb went off in the place. Miraculously, no one was killed or seriously injured. There was extensive damage to the walls, which were pockmarked from shrapnel, and some blood on the floor; but that was all.

Coincidentally, I was in a restaurant shortly before the coup about two buildings down when the blast occurred. I was having lunch with one of our OSI agents who was visiting us from Thailand. He was kidding me about the quietness of Saigon and thought we were "pushing it" to accept combat pay. I was trying to point out to him that guerrilla warfare was like that. One day everything was quiet and the next explosions are occurring everywhere. Almost in tune with my statement, the explosion shook the building and brought down pictures and tableware. My friend from Bangkok turned white and asked what we should do. I told him to stay there. One thing you don't do after an explosion is to stick your head out the window to see what it was. Frequently, the VC would plant two bombs to go off almost simultaneously, the second going off just a few minutes after the first.

The floating restaurant that I've referred to earlier, where Bill Griffies and I had a little problem with a Frenchman, was subject to just such a tactic a few years later. Midday, a bicycle bomb went off on the dock near the floating restaurant. Almost immediately after the explosion, a second bomb went off, just when diners had jumped up and were attempting to get off the restaurant.

In that attack, several people were killed and a number seriously injured. The bicycle bomb had been a tactic used by the North Vietnamese against the French by the communist Viet Minh. It was ideally suited to Vietnam. Bicycles were the chief means of transportation in both North and South Vietnam. They were all over the country and checking them would be an impossible task.

The bicycle bomb was made by stuffing plastic explosive into the hollow frame and attaching a timer and detonating device. It could also be command detonated by fastening an electrical detonator in the plastic explosive and running a wire to an electrical source. The bicycle would explode into many pieces of shrapnel. It was a simple but very effective terrorist weapon. Some protection was afforded when signs warned people not to place their bicycles next to store fronts or windows. But, with the thousands of bicycles in Saigon, it was almost impossible to enforce these precautions. Another tactic was to place an innocent looking package on a table or chair. If on a table, it would explode at about waist level causing injury to people sitting at tables.

For weeks we had been getting information that the Kinh Do Theater, located in Saigon and catering to Americans was a bombing target of the VC. More than one source alerted us to this possible attack. At the time there were a few civilians and dependents still in Saigon. Going to the Kinh Do was one of the few pleasures that they could enjoy. After several warnings, MACV placed a lone military policeman at the entrance. A favorite time to go to the movies was on the weekends and Saturday was one of the busiest days.

Bill Griffies talked me into going to the movie. The feature was a murder mystery named *The List of Adrian*

Messenger. I was to meet Bill there just before the show started. I was a little hungry and opened a can of peanuts. As I did so, I cut my finger rather deeply. I had difficulty stopping the flow of blood. Concerned, I walked around the corner to the Rex Bachelor Officer's Quarters (BOQ). It had a small dispensary with a medical corpsman. I went in and the corpsman cleaned and bandaged my finger. Just as he was finishing the dressing a tremendous explosion occurred nearby. "The Kinh Do" I thought. I ran out and got in my car and took off for the theater.

When I arrived at the theater, there were several ambulances already there. A large cloud of dust surrounded the building. I looked over on the steps to the entrance and saw the body of the young military policeman. He was lying facedown and a red splotch on his back indicated that he had been shot in the back. I noticed that his pistol was missing from his holster and was nowhere in sight. People were staggering out of the theater covered with dust and some bleeding profusely. Bill Griffies was nowhere in sight and I was concerned that he might have been injured. Suddenly, I spotted Jene Hunter. He was wearing a white sport shirt the front of which was covered with blood.

He had gone back into the theater to rescue a woman who had been cut by glass down her front and her face. He said that there was a lot of loose concrete just hanging there waiting to fall on someone. His shirt front was bloody from flying glass caused by the initial explosion. He nevertheless went back in to help someone who needed it.

Four of the people who worked in my CI division were in the theater and were all injured. Most of their injuries were from falling debris from the ceiling. Jene Hunter and the four men all were to later receive the Purple Heart, the decoration awarded to people who have been wounded in combat. Bill Griffies had not gone in the theater. He had waited out front for me. He heard a shot and looked up and saw the body of the policeman just as the explosion occurred. He did not see the VC, but observed a bullet hole in the windshield of his car. While he did not see what happened, he thought that the policeman had gotten his gun out and fired a shot before he died. This would have been after he was shot and that is why the shot went wild and into the parking area.

Later we would find out that there was another hero involved besides the young military policeman. When the VC tossed the explosives into the back of the theater, a young Marine officer saw them and realizing what was happening yelled out for everyone to "Hit the deck." He was killed by the blast as he stood up to warn everyone. No doubt, he saved many lives by giving the warning. He and the policeman were the only ones killed but many people were injured both by the blast and falling debris. The VC who carried out the attack escaped without anyone identifying them.

Shortly after the Kinh Do bombing a USAF aircraft, carrying flares for support of outposts, exploded right after taking off. All crewmembers were killed. OSI immediately went to the aircraft's organization to investigate. This incident pointed out the difference in environments existing between investigation in the US and in a guerrilla war. The plane exploded only a few miles away from the base as it was taking off on a mission.

Debris was scattered throughout the jungle surrounding the base. It would be impossible to examine the debris to determine the exact cause of the explosion.

OSI interviewed all ground crew members and found that there was nothing unusual observed. Since the aircraft contained flares, there was a possibility that a flare had exploded accidentally and caused the others to explode. This had never happened before and appeared to be unlikely. No gunfire was heard or observed in the vicinity of the aircraft. The aircraft was one of several which were airborne each night. If an outpost was attacked by the VC at night, the outpost called in the flare ship. The flares that would be dropped would completely illuminate the area surrounding the outpost. Often, the flare ship would be accompanied by the AC47, a transport heavily armed, which could bring down tremendous fire into a small area. The armed transports were called "Puff the Magic Dragon" and were very effective in preventing successful VC attacks at night.

OSI received information that indicated that a US civilian, employed by the US Government, might be engaged in espionage. The person was engaged in a classified project of great importance and was known to have been seen in the company of a Polish officer assigned to the International Control Commission (ICC). That officer had been identified as an intelligence agent. The ICC was actually part of the International Commission for Supervision and Control (ICSC). It was a body established by the 1954 Geneva Conference to oversee the observance of the armistice agreements in Vietnam, Cambodia and Laos. The ICSC was made up of India as the Chairman and Canada and Poland as members. The ICS tried to determine to what extent the guerrilla war was the result of actions taken by North Vietnam. In 1962, it issued a report condemning North Vietnam for escalating the VC guerrilla war, with Poland objecting,

The ICSC teams could travel, unimpeded to Laos, Cambodia and Vietnam, including both North and South Vietnam. The team was not popular with North or South Vietnam, but was able to travel about freely. The Polish officer on the team had become acquainted with the American suspect through encounters in Saigon. All Americans had been briefed that they were to report any contact with Soviet Bloc citizens. The suspect in this case did not report his association with the Polish officer. He was therefore made the subject of an espionage investigation. We conducted a complete review of his background investigation and found nothing derogatory. He was a well-educated person who worked in a technical specialty for the USAF. He lived in Saigon and was also employed there. The investigation was initiated by requesting CIA to set up a 24 hour surveillance on him off-base. OSI would establish coverage of his activities on-base.

The investigation did not get off to a good start. After about a month of negative reports from CIA on his off-base activities, we discovered that CIA had set up its surveillance on the wrong house. We wondered what his activities were during that month when CIA was watching the wrong residence, and asked them to verify the correct address before continuing with the surveillance. The address system in Saigon was a hodge-podge and probably accounted for surveillance on the wrong residence. After several more weeks of surveillance at both home and work, we found that the suspect had not been in contact with the Polish agent, nor had he done anything suspicious or out of the ordinary.

After receiving word from OSI Headquarters, we called the suspect in for interrogation. He was completely cooperative and said that he had been studying Polish and practiced it when he met the Polish officer for dinner on a few occasions. He said that he did not report the contact because he felt that whom he associated with during non working hours was his business. This comment was inappropriate for someone who dealt with highly classified information on a daily basis. A search of his residence had revealed nothing of significance.

Based on his comment about his time being his own, we asked for and got permission to run him on the lie detector. I questioned the ability of the lie detector operator and his total lack of CI experience, but we proceeded with the examination anyway. According to the results presented to me by the operator, the suspect had passed the test and was believed to have answered all the questions truthfully. The agency that he worked for immediately transferred him back to the US because they did not feel that he was mature enough to deal with classified matters. I had been involved a few times with lie detector examinations and did not value them very highly. They could be fooled and later events proved this. People can be trained to be resistant to the lie detector. Even today (2004) US courts do not allow the results of lie detector tests to be admissible, except under very narrow and limited circumstances. Despite the unreliability of such tests, even today the FBI, NSA and the CIA rely heavily on them. Aldridge Ames, the CIA traitor was able to successfully convince the operator that his answers were truthful despite the fact that he was a long-time Soviet spy.

One incident occurred during my tour in Vietnam convinced me that inter-service rivalry was a serious problem. I was contacted by an Army captain who was the Operations Officer for an Army helicopter squadron. He said that the squadron was engaged in "Eagle Flights." These were flights of about sixteen US Army helicopters which carried about 100 Vietnamese Rangers. They would descend on villages in the Mekong Delta, surround them and then shakedown everyone in the village in an attempt to identify any VC. The helicopters were flown by US Army crewmen and each carried an array of rockets and machine guns.

Often, as a result of such operations, they would pick up suspected or confirmed VC. The problem was that they never found out what happened to the suspects after they were turned over to the South Vietnamese. I asked if they had requested support from Army Intelligence and was told that they would not go out on any of these missions. The captain wanted to know if OSI could send an agent out on an Eagle Flight and determine what happened to people captured as a result of the operation. I told him that I would check with my boss and see if we could assist the Army by sending someone out on a mission. I spoke to Colonel Sharpe and suggested that it might be a way to establish some rapport with the Army and may possibly result in some information about VC activity. He said that there was some danger involved and that no one could be ordered to go on such a mission. I told him that I would ask for a volunteer. I had two junior officers and five enlisted agents assigned to my CI division and felt that one would be interested in doing something positive.

To my surprise, neither of my two officers wanted to go out on the mission. I did not think that I wanted to ask my enlisted agents to volunteer when the two officers would not. I reported to Colonel Sharpe that I could not find a volunteer. He agreed that I should not ask the enlisted agents if none of the officers would go out. The colonel said that there was one other solution, if I felt that we should send someone out. He said that I could go on the mission. I agreed that I would be willing to go and then contacted the Army captain and told him that I would be going out on the mission. He said that he would call me the day before the next mission and that the flights took off early in the morning. He said to be sure and come armed, a suggestion that I did not need.

Within a couple of days, I received a call informing me that the mission would be the following day and that I was to be at the helicopter pad by 06.00 A.M. He would be there to introduce me to the crew that I would fly with and give me a short briefing.

I acknowledged that I would be there. He reminded me that the flight was classified and that I should not mention it to anyone outside of the OSI. I went to bed that evening somewhat apprehensive about the next day. I was about to experience something that might be dangerous and it made me feel fear for the first time, since I had been in Vietnam.

A young sergeant, who worked at OSI Headquarters insisted on drawing my weapon and taking me to the helicopter pad the next morning. When I arrived at my office early the next day, the sergeant was waiting for me. He said he had obtained ammunition and an AR15 rifle. The fear that I had felt the previous day was gone.

I concentrated on what I was to do and, as an after-thought, I had taken my 35 mm camera with me. The sergeant drove me to the part of Tan Son Nhut where the Eagle Flights took off, and when we arrived we saw the sixteen helicopters lined up. We parked and the sergeant opened the trunk of the car. I looked in and there were two AR15 rifles in it. I looked at the sergeant and he said, "Sir, I am not letting you go alone." "I am going with you."

I told him that he couldn't go out with me. He was not even an agent. He was an administrative airman and his usual weapon was a typewriter. I replied that he was not going. I looked at him and saw the resolution in his face. Suddenly, I felt that if I got into a tight spot, I wanted this young sergeant with me. I figured if anything happened to him it would also happen to me and I would not have to worry about any repercussions. The Army captain appeared and directed us to a helicopter. It would be the prisoner chopper. It would remove any prisoners from the area and not land unless there were prisoners taken. We were to fly at about 600 feet and at about eighty miles per hour. The first village that we would hit was about thirty miles south of Saigon. We would hit two other villages after the initial strike on the first village.

As we went south, we had only been out for about twenty minutes when I saw a village flying the VC flag. I tapped the pilot, who was an Army warrant officer, as was the co-pilot, and pointed down at the village. He shook his head, letting me know that we were not going anywhere near that village. The Vietnamese had chosen the villages that we would hit and that was not one of them. I was surprised to see the VC flag flying from a village that was less than fifty miles from Saigon. We continued on and skirted the village, not indicating that we knew it was there.

About fifteen minutes after passing the first village, we climbed up a few feet and watched as the other helicopters descended in a semicircle and started disgorging Vietnamese Rangers. They moved through the shoulder high grass leaving a visible trail of flattened grass. Within minutes, we started to descend toward the village. We could see women and children running in all directions as we flew over the village. There were no men in sight. The village was possibly contributing to the VC by providing its men.

When we landed the chopper we saw a Vietnamese, dressed in the traditional black pajama like garment and wearing a khaki hat. He was trembling and appeared to weigh not more than ninety pounds. He reminded me of a small boy, though he was probably in his forties. He was being treated quite roughly by the Vietnamese Rangers; but they stopped roughing him up when they saw us approaching. He was placed in our chopper and we took off for a destination that only the pilot knew. A few minutes later we set down in a clearing where there were two Vietnamese policemen waiting. The man was blindfolded, had his hands tied behind his back and was forced to kneel on the ground. We flew away with that being our last view of the man. The police watched us as we departed. We had no idea of what was going to happen to him. The highest ranking American on the mission was a Lieutenant Colonel, while the highest ranking Vietnamese was a lieutenant. Apparently, their idea of leadership was not the same as ours. While we sent out a Lieutenant Colonel they chose to send, as the senior officer, a junior officer.

Suddenly, we were directed to another village, the second one apparently being free of any recognizable VC. After flying for about fifteen minutes, we descended to what appeared to be the outskirts of a small village. The land was marshy and our chopper set down in the water, which came up about a foot above the ground. As we set down, I observed a sudden movement to my right. A man came out of the water, where he apparently had been hiding. I turned my weapon toward him and found that my safety was on and I couldn't fire. Almost instantly, a Vietnamese Ranger came from behind and grabbed the man and, placing his arms behind his back, and forced him on to the floor of our chopper.

I noticed two things as that event transpired. First, I looked down at the man and he had a fresh haircut that was very neatly done and second, the Vietnamese Ranger was carrying a Thompson submachine gun that was so filthy that I was relieved that he hadn't fired it. The prisoner's hands were securely tied behind him and he lay on the floor as our chopper took off again. I could tell by his appearance that we had caught ourselves a real VC. He was about in his mid-twenties and was expressionless. As we left the area, he showed no fear or any other emotion. He had broad shoulders and appeared to be in excellent physical condition. Shortly, we were at another landing site and the first scene repeated itself. Two Vietnamese policemen were waiting as the ranger pulled him from the chopper. He too was placed on his knees and was in that position, with the two policemen standing over him, as we flew away. The choppers turned back toward Saigon and shortly we were landing back at Tan Son Nhut on the pad that we had departed from. The Operations Officer was not there, so the sergeant and I placed our weapons back in the trunk of the car and departed for our office.

What followed was a disaster. A few days later, we were preparing our Significant Counterintelligence Brief

(SCIB). It was usually about thirty pages and detailed what of significance occurred during the past month. It was disseminated locally to the Army and the embassy as well as being sent back to OSI Headquarters. Instantly, there was a response from the Army. The captain who had arranged my flight was told that he would never again allow an Air Force officer to participate in any operations. It appeared that my report had embarrassed the Army when it showed that all that effort resulted in the capture of one possible VC and one not too likely VC. I felt sorry for the captain who was severely criticized for trying to do his job.

My turn was next. I was called to his office by General Anthis and, not in a very pleasant way, he said that he did not want me to give the US Army one reason for being in Vietnam. I was not to have anything to do with Army people from then on. He must have felt, unlike the Army, that I had somehow helped in their effort. Finally, Colonel Sharpe received a message from OSI Headquarters condemning my action and he was told that OSI did not go out on combat missions. They asked in sort of a postscript whether or not I was in uniform and whether or not I carried my OSI credentials. Hopefully, they were somewhat pacified when Colonel Sharpe advised them that I was in uniform and that I only carried an Air Force ID card. It was the talk of the Headquarters, and not favorable talk at that, until the Director of OSI, General Cappucci, who had been in intelligence during World War II, opined that it was a gutsy thing to do and he was proud of me. No more discussion ensued about my poor judgment after the General's comments.

The last time I heard anything about the Army helicopter regiment was when I was called upon to brief some OSI colonel. We frequently borrowed a slide projector from the USAF hospital when we needed to give a briefing. I was standing in the hall waiting for the projector when in came two stretchers, one was taken into the operating room immediately. I could see that the young man's right shoulder looked like something had taken a bite out of it. He appeared to be in extreme pain as they forced him down on the operating table. When they closed the door to the operating room, I looked down on the other stretcher that had been placed at my feet and saw a young black soldier who was crying like a baby. The medic who had helped bring them in said that they had been in a helicopter that was shot down by the VC. The man in the operating room had been hit with a bullet in his right shoulder, the other young fellow had broken his back when the chopper crashed. Suddenly, I realized that this war was real and though the violence was not always apparent to those of us not directly engaged in combat, it was always there and could manifest itself at any time.

During the next twelve months, there were a total of seven coups. Governments changed so fast it was impossible to effect any liaison with host security and intelligence agencies. Despite US appeals, the South Vietnamese could not find a government that they could follow. The governments were usually headed by Generals who changed into civilian clothes, but lost none of their military rigidity.

We were there to assist the South Vietnamese in preventing a communist takeover of their country. They did not want our advice and only wanted financial assistance. I never saw or heard of Major Trong again. I was told that he had been transferred to the Central Highlands. His successor changed three times in as many months. Our collection efforts were pretty much limited to the Embassy and the CIA. Like us though, they did not know how to deal with a constantly changing government which had to establish itself each time there was a change.

When I first arrived in South Vietnam I attended an interdepartmental security meeting at the US Embassy. It was chaired by the embassy Security Officer. I remembered that at the first meeting I attended one of the subjects was opening the road to Cap St. Jacques, a beach resort southeast of Saigon. No one was allowed to go there without a military escort, usually consisting of Army Military Police in half-tracks. The Vietnamese, who saw the monetary advantage of an influx of off duty Americans, were pressing the American Embassy to open the road and allow free travel.

All the representatives of the military that were present voted against the idea. One officer pointed out that anyone traveling on the road to Cap St. Jacques would be vulnerable to VC action, since there were no military units in the immediate vicinity. After everyone present had given their opinion, all of them negative, the Security Officer said, "Sorry, gentlemen, I see no danger to using the road; it is important to the province chief, whom we are trying to get along with, and I am going to recommend to the ambassador that the road be opened."

Three days after that meeting, a young airman, driving a gasoline truck from Saigon to Bien Hoa, got lost and ended up on the road to Cap St. Jacques. He was promptly captured by the VC and his gasoline truck destroyed by fire. That seemed to dispose of the question as to the safety of the road for US travel. When my tour was about over, I attended another meeting of the

121

Interdepartmental Security Group and the first topic to be discussed was whether or not we should open the road to Cap St. Jacques. Everyone present agreed that the road should not be opened. Strangely, there was no comment from the Security Officer. The subject was closed, apparently for another year.

As my tour drew to a close, I felt a feeling of frustration and also a lack of any sense of accomplishment. During the last year I had tried to work with the US Army and the CIA as well as the South Vietnamese security services. No permanent relationships had been established and we had to almost totally rely on getting information from anyone who might feel like giving it at the time. I saw no significant progress in the war in which we were supporting, at best, an indifferent ally. The maneuvering of each military service to become predominant led to sub-optimization of our efforts.

One thing I had learned was that the role of CI in guerrilla warfare, while retaining the original goals, had to adjust its operating procedures to conform to the needs of that type of warfare. In a guerrilla war, the CI effort must be directed against the guerrillas directly. This can only be done by fielding CI operatives who can develop sources and institute CI operations right in the guerrillas' backyard. The counter-guerrilla operations in the Philippines instituted by President Magsaysay were successful because the operatives were natives who knew the country and spoke the language. Supplied by the US with arms and equipment, the Filipino Government placed the guerrillas at a distinct disadvantage and finally defeated them. In South Vietnam, we never developed any capability to venture beyond the safety of our bases. We never trained and required the South Vietnamese to aggressively operate a CI program.

I was returning to the US with a pessimistic view of our chances for success in Vietnam. I knew that this attitude was unpopular with both the US Government and the US military. The feeling that we were doing well and about to "see the light at the end of the tunnel" was the only acceptable view and my experiences had taught me that there had been no real progress and any progress that was achieved was totally wiped out by the constant changes in the South Vietnamese Government, as well as its resistance to any US suggestions for conducting the war. There was, I thought, a feeling among the US military, that if we were to bring American troops into the war, our high-tech weaponry and superior mobility would quickly win the contest. General Westmoreland, who was the commander at the time was already asking for more troops and assuring the President that the war would be won quickly. I was ready to leave.

What puzzled me was the fact that American conventional firepower, if it was to be used, would be directed at an enemy which fought at a time and place of its choosing and did not seek to take and hold land. The goal of the VC and the North Vietnamese was to win over the minds of their fellow Vietnamese in South Vietnam. Their effort was aided by the long history of a totally dictatorial regime, which was isolated from the populace. Diem's recent demise did little to change the attitudes of the populace. The US answer to this dilemma was to pour more and more money into the country and gradually expand American military participation. It seemed that the optimism of the US Government was unbounded, despite the failures both politically and militarily. Each day, our casualty list increased.

RETURN TO HEADQUARTERS

It was August, 1964 and I was heading back to the United States. I had been reassigned back to OSI Headquarters; in fact I was to be in my old job, analyst for PACAF. The new Section Chief, for whom I would be working, was Brewer Newton. I felt fortunate to be working for him again and looked forward to it. I would still be handling the Vietnam desk, only this time I would have the benefit of having been there and experienced the war first hand.

When I reported to headquarters, it seemed that nothing had changed. Everyone was enjoying the slower pace and many of the same people who were there when I left, were still there. There was little interest in Vietnam and I was asked few questions by other agents. I was to brief the General on the war at his staff meeting and answer any questions that were presented by his staff.

I began my presentation by pointing out that the country was in a mess with the constant coups and countercoups. I described the difficulty encountered in conducting CI under the circumstances of a countrywide guerrilla war. We were supposed to be advising the Vietnamese, but they did not take advice. While there were no US combat forces in-country at the time, I felt that the only way of winning would be to defeat the VC in battle and the South Vietnamese had shown that they could not or would not do what was necessary. Up to that time we had only about 300 people killed in Vietnam, and I felt that we would lose more as it continued.

My briefing was not well received by the General or

his staff. Finally, I was asked by one of his staff members, what I thought would be necessary to win the war. I replied that only with the introduction of American combat troops could any progress be made: I did not know whether or not we would win, but our chances would be greatly improved. The same individual asked sarcastically, "Do you really think that we would send American boys over there to fight their war?" I replied that I did not know, but it would take a couple of hundred thousand troops if we were to make a serious effort.

I left the briefing feeling that the whole year I was in Vietnam was wasted. No one believed in my assessment of the situation and I began to feel that perhaps I was wrong and that there had been progress in the war and I was not aware of it. Later on, I was asked to brief the General on other countries that I handled, but he never asked for a briefing at his staff meeting on Vietnam. I had private talks with him when I had occasion to go to his office, but he never believed that my pessimistic description of the situation could be correct. After all, the President had said that we were not going to send American boys to fight in an Asian war. But, that was exactly what we planned to do. One year later, we would have about 140,000 US combat troops in South Vietnam and financial as well as military support increased significantly. With the introduction of US troops our casualty list grew longer and our financial support became astronomical. With the increases, came increased optimism on the part of the US Government.

I had only been back three months when OSI decided to set up a class in CI for members of the VNAF. I was selected to go as an instructor in *Sabotage and Espionage*. I was very unhappy about it, but was told that the course needed experienced agents and I was one of them. I arrived back in South Vietnam in November 1964 and was met by members of the local OSI Office. I was taken to a really raunchy hotel and told that it was the best they could get for me. They explained that there were now 140,000 US in the country and the South Korean "Tiger Division" was arriving that day. I was told that all the teaching materials had arrived and that instruction would begin the following Monday. The class would consist of sixteen South Vietnamese airmen, who supposedly all spoke English. One bright spot was the fact that I would teach during the third week and that was all. That meant that I could be on my way home in three weeks.

The classes took place without any difficulty. Since all the students said "Yes" to everything I said, I was not certain just how much they understood. The assignment ended without any problems. One matter of note, we had trained the class in the use of .38 cal. pistols, and shortly after the course, one of the students distinguished himself by shooting and wounding a Vietnamese civilian in a bar brawl. If they could be as aggressive with the VC as they were with Vietnamese civilians then our efforts would not have been wasted. I left Vietnam, again with serious doubts as to whether or not we were accomplishing anything of lasting importance.

My second tour at the headquarters was very different from my first. I was considered an experienced agent and was given numerous "specials" to run, principally for the Chief of Staff of the USAF, that is, for the Office of the Chief of Staff. Almost all the investigations involved "leaks." Leaks were the release of classified information to the media by "person or persons" unknown. Leaking was one of the favorite pastimes of many of the higher ranking military and government bureaucrats. It was a well-established phenomenon. While everyone decried the leaking of classified information, it was often done by those who criticized it the most. As I write this, in October, 2002, I see on the news that Secretary of Defense Rumsfeld has complained about a leak concerning the US operational concept for attacking Iraq. This is one of several leaks that the present Administration has had to face.

Leaks occur for several reasons. First, if a person does not agree with some action that is being planned, he can leak it to the media and perhaps publicize it so that it will be abandoned. Second, leaks can occur simply to damage the credibility or effectiveness of the person originating the information. Third, leaks can occur by the people who originate the information. The leak can be a trial balloon to see if certain planned actions will be acceptable, or to gain insight into public reaction to a planned action. This latter leak is made by policymakers, usually high up in government or the military. Leaks are a potent weapon for disgruntled military, whose position does not allow them to publicly disagree with the Administration on matters of policy or some planned action. Civilian members of the Department of Defense also engaged in the practice. Aside from causing embarrassment to some people it seemed that leaks did little long term damage.

The investigation of leaks became an important part of my experiences after I returned from Vietnam. I was summoned to the General's office and told that the Department of Defense Inspector General (IG) wanted support from OSI in the conduct of investigations that were of great importance to the Secretary of Defense. I was told that I was going to be sent over to the Pentagon to work on behalf of the IG. The supervisor was to be a high-ranking civilian named Donald Stewart, who was the IG's Director of Investigations. That was all I was told. I was to report to Mr. Stewart the next day.

I asked around and was told that Donald Stewart was an ex- FBI agent who had moved over to the Department of Defense. He was considered highly professional, extremely good at what he did and had little patience with fools and incompetents.

The next day I reported to the Pentagon and was directed to Don Stewart's office. I met Don Stewart and we had a brief discussion. He was not pleased with some of the military investigators that had been sent in the past. He wanted people who were professional and self-starters. People who had to constantly be told what the next step in an investigation was were of little use to him. He wanted people who could think for themselves and work without constantly asking for guidance or requiring supervision.

We went over the list of people who had been given access to the leaked document. We divided up the list and started to interview those people. Don pointed out that the leak had been to Bill Beecher of *The New York Times*. He mentioned that under no circumstances were we to interview Beecher or any member of the press. We were to try and establish if anyone would acknowledge acquaintanceship or association with Bill Beecher.

One of the major difficulties associated with the investigation of leaks was determining the scope, that is who actually had access to the leaked document. While it was true that documents were supposed to be limited to certain officials, it was also true that the documents were seen by secretaries and staff members who worked for the actual recipients of the documents. So it was very likely that documents sent to only sixty people may have been seen and/or handled by twice that number. The first step was always trying to determine who, in addition to the intended receiver, also had access to the document. Reviewing the original document received was a second step. Notations on it or other writings might reveal distribution and access.

It was necessary to interview everyone who ostensibly had access to the document. During that particular investigation, Don Stewart found out that Beecher had been given a pass to the General Officer's Mess and could actually eat in close proximity to where the high ranking officers had their meals. The IG, a three-star General, immediately canceled the pass and wrote a directive stating that the names of all non-Department of Defense civilians given a pass to the General's Mess would be given to his office and the name of their sponsors would also be given.

After a few days of interviews, I came across a US Navy captain who had been given access to the leaked information. After discussing his duties with him I asked him if he was acquainted with William Beecher of *The New York Times*. To my surprise, he answered yes to the question. I asked if he had a social or business relationship with Beecher. He replied that he had both a business and a social relationship. He seemed to be very proud of this relationship. I asked, "Was he ever authorized to release classified information to anyone?" He replied that he was not. I asked him when the last time was that he had been in contact with Beecher. He stated that Beecher had been a dinner guest in his home during the last week and I asked him bluntly, "Did you ever discuss the document in question with Beecher?" He said, "Bill Beecher knows better than to try and get any information out of me. We have discussions because he values my intellect, but he has never asked me any questions about classified information." I asked him, "In these discussions, don't you rely on information that you receive on your job?" He gave me a surprised look and said, "I don't believe that I should say any more to you."

I reported the interview and Don informed me that all the people on our list had been interviewed and the captain was the only one who admitted being acquainted with Beecher. Don reported to the Secretary of Defense and we were told to stop the investigation. The Secretary had gotten the information he wanted. Within a week the captain had been transferred to San Diego, California to a supply facility. We had not proven beyond a reasonable doubt that the captain was the leaker; but we had proven it to the satisfaction of Secretary of Defense, Melvin Laird.

When it came to classified materials, no chances could be taken. Anyone who was considered unreliable in protecting such information had to be refused access.

Often, denial of access would have a limiting effect on a person's career, because higher rank required higher responsibility and this included responsibility for handling classified information.

One case that Don Stewart and I worked on turned out to be an investigator's dream. A document that was generated by the Department of Defense had been leaked to Congress. The document purported to show that in negotiating with Spain for the leases on the bases that we had there, we were paying them much more money than we announced publicly. This document could do nothing but embarrass the Department of Defense and irritate our Spanish allies. Even worse, the document was not complete. The document's distribution was extremely limited. We saw an excellent opportunity to solve this leak. After checking several offices, I went to the Office of a Deputy Assistant Secretary of Defense and asked to see his copy.

The Secretary of Defense was a former Congressman and the leak had been brought to his attention by a former aide, who sent him a copy of the document that Congress had received. We had noticed that when the document had been copied to be sent to Congress, it had a large paper clip on the upper right corner. When the Deputy Assistant Secretary produced his copy of the document, there was the large paper clip. It had not changed position. I excused myself and called Don Stewart. Don came down to the Deputy's office and informed him that the document had definitely been leaked from his office. The Deputy did not show any reaction to the revelation. Don Stewart asked who in the office had access to that document. The names of nine naval officers were given us. According to the Deputy, these people had been involved in the drafting of the document and had access to the completed document.

We returned to Don's office and without any discussion, we both commented that the Deputy was a good suspect. The document had been retained in his office. Don briefed the Secretary of Defense and he asked if we wanted to consider polygraphing the naval officers involved. Don suggested that we just ask each of them if they would be willing to submit to a lie detector examination. The next day we called them all in and asked them. One said that he would not take the exam, "on principle." When we reported the results of our inquiry to the Secretary he advised us that the Deputy Secretary had just submitted his resignation. It was immediately accepted by the Secretary. He thanked us for our efforts and instructed us to close the investigation.

When I had returned to OSI after the completion of that "special" OSI received a letter signed by the Lieutenant General who was IG of the Department of Defense and Don's boss. It thanked me for my outstanding performance and investigative skill in conducting a sensitive, high-level investigation. I knew that the letter had been written by Don Stewart. He always took care of the people who performed well for him and I received numerous other such letters for later investigations. These letters were of great benefit to my career and were greatly appreciated.

The investigations were important; even though they were conducted after the fact, because it was important to detect and punish those who had no respect for national security and who placed it second to their petty dislikes and ambitions. Unfortunately, many leakers are not caught. The Pentagon, like many other government offices, has entirely too many reproduction machines and too wide a dissemination of sensitive documents. Many people unfortunately, do not consider careless or improper handling of classified material a serious offense. Using your birthday date as a safe combination, using the birthdates of your wife or children for safe combinations, and using your social security number, are all careless ways to handle classified material. Copy machines can be configured to require identification before they can be used. If it is important enough, copy machines can be rigged to photograph everything that is copied. No measure can completely prevent copying sensitive documents for leaking; but perhaps increasing the penalty could reduce such practices.

I went to the Pentagon one day to consult with an Air Force colonel who was a key planner on the Air Staff. The colonel told me that the investigation that I was to undertake was Top Secret and sensitive. He explained that the USAF had installed a station in Sam Neua Province in Laos, near the border of North Vietnam. It was placed on a mountain top which had extremely sheer cliffs around three sides of it and it had a flat summit. Helicopters could be landed on the site, which was code named "Lima Site 85." The purpose of this secret redoubt was to contain what is called a Tactical Air Control and Navigation (TACAN) beacon which guided USAF jets to targets in the Red River Delta in North Vietnam. In March, 1968, North Vietnamese and Pathet Lao forces attacked that site and overran it. Several Americans were killed, the site was lost to the North Vietnamese and the TACAN equipment was destroyed. The beacon had allowed American bombers to fly into the Hanoi-Haiphong areas and bomb accurately even under the worst weather conditions. Its loss was serious and the suspicion that its location had been compromised called for an investigation. The knowledge concerning the location and purpose of the site was, necessarily, possessed by many people There was also a possibility that the North Vietnamese may have discovered the site. They had troops in the immediate area who might have observed the site.

The officers in the Air Staff felt that the site had been compromised, possibly by someone in the United States. The training base for the people who operated the site was in the western United States and all personnel who were involved in the operation went through training there. Also, the movement to and from the site was by helicopter and it was a short flight time from the site to secure territory. Because of the mountainous area in which the site was located, only a helicopter could get in and out. When the weather was inclement, the helicopters could not get in.

The day the site was attacked by the North Vietnamese was a foggy, rainy day and the helicopters could not get into the site. There was a warning of imminent attack but the US State Department held off any rescue attempt until it was too late. It was a judgment that was harmful to the people who manned the site. Several of the people on the site were killed by the North Vietnamese. Because of the secret nature of the operation, there was little publicity about the action. Only the parents and loved ones of the people killed grieved at their loss. As in other areas of the Vietnam War, civilians were given control over military operations without any responsibility for their actions.

I was told that there was a good suspect, in the United States, who may have compromised the site location. The wife of one of the sergeants, who had served a tour on the site, was working in a service industry and allegedly discussed the site with her clients. The location and mission of the site were classified. Some of the wives of other men who had served on the site complained about this woman's gossiping about the operation.

I immediately flew to the west coast and went to the facility where the training was taking place. I discovered, when I arrived there, that the woman and her husband had been transferred to a radar site in Saskatchewan,

Canada. The most precise location that I was given was about thirty miles north of the city of Regina, Saskatchewan. I called the Pentagon and spoke with the colonel who had dispatched me to the west coast. When I told him of the move, he said, "OK, go after them." I immediately boarded a plane for Calgary, Canada and from there I flew to Regina. I rented a car and proceeded north from Regina. I had no idea how I was going to locate the couple. There was supposedly no town close by where they lived.

I had been driving for about an hour when, suddenly, I saw off to the left of the road, an American flag flying from a small mobile home. I pulled over to ask questions and to my surprise, it was the home of the couple I had been seeking. The sergeant was at home and I identified myself to him and his wife and then informed them of the purpose for my visit. The sergeant was not happy to see me and eyed his wife suspiciously after I explained the purpose of my visit.

The wife was a pretty, young woman who acted very young for her age, twenty two. I interviewed her and asked her if she had ever discussed the mission and/or the location of the operating site. She immediately denied ever discussing the subject with anyone. She burst into tears and repeated her denials. I watched her husband and he seemed unsympathetic to her situation. I asked had her gossiping ever been a problem between them. He lost his composure and started berating her and stating that she had promised not to indulge in gossip. It obviously had been a problem.

I asked her if she remembered a group of Soviets traveling through the town near where they were stationed. She said that she had no recollection of such a visit.

Then, it was like I turned on a tap. She started telling about the affairs of everyone that was stationed there. It seemed as if she could not stop herself. She knew everyone's personal affairs and spoke of them at length. Her husband was seething and I decided it was time for me to leave. I believed that I had gotten the answers that I came for.

I flew to Las Vegas and then went to the OSI Office nearby and called the colonel. I told him that there was definitely a problem, but that I could not confirm that her gossip reached any Soviets who might have overheard her. When I returned to Washington, DC I learned that the sergeant had been immediately reassigned to less sensitive duty, an action that would not aid his career advancement.

When I returned to Washington, DC the Chief of the Special Activities Branch called me into his office and announced that the Republican National Convention was going to be held in Miami, Florida, at the Jackie Gleason Auditorium. The Secret Service was undermanned and had requested that OSI provide agents trained in DVP to provide support. We had only a few weeks to send an advance team to Miami and coordinate the operation with the Secret Service. I was to effect initial coordination and act as liaison between the OSI and the Secret Service. OSI was also to identify Technical Agents who would set up a radio communications network.

The next day I was to attend a Secret Service briefing that was being given to the Secret Service agents who would be involved. The meeting seemed to be more motivational than instructive. Rufus Youngblood, the agent who had thrown himself on Lyndon Johnson during the Kennedy assassination appeared to address the group and was welcomed like a rock star. The agents displayed a tremendous spirit of teamwork. They all seemed aware of the fact that all the Republican candidates for President were to be given protection coverage and that it would be a major effort.

Over 100 OSI agents were selected to assist the Secret Service in providing the protection coverage. The agents who were selected were promptly notified and alerted to prepare for departure to Miami at any time. I went to meet the Secret Service agent who would mange the operation and was given a briefing on OSI's role. The Secret Service would have their command post set up in the Fontainebleau Hotel; OSI's command post would be in the Saxony Hotel, which was located some distance away from the Fontainebleau. The Secret Service was to man all the internal posts in the various places the candidates were staying. OSI agents would be assigned to external coverage, which would involve stationary street posts and vehicle patrols. The outdoor temperatures in Miami were in the high ninety degrees and the heat would be a definite limiting factor for our agents. We set up a procedure of having our agents work three hour shifts instead of longer ones. They would have to be on duty more often, but for shorter periods. All our agents were to be armed and only those who were qualified with the pistol were selected. We did not have to disqualify one man.

When I arrived in Miami, I went directly to the Fontainebleau Hotel to coordinate with the chief agent. I asked him if they had photographed Miami Beach from the air to show all the entrances to the hotels involved. He looked at me in disbelief. I told him not to worry; we would take care of it. That afternoon, I spent one hour in a US Marine helicopter, photographing all of the hotels on the beach. Thanks to the photo laboratory at Homestead Air Force Base, by early evening both the Secret Service and OSI had over 160 aerial photographs of the hotels. All of their entrances and outbuildings were shown as were all roads and beach areas. When I delivered the photographs the Secret Service agent said nothing. He did not need to comment, our professionalism spoke for itself.

Our first problem was setting up the radio communications network; the high buildings diminished our signals and limited our range. We set up a relay system so that by contacting nearby cars our agents could relay their messages to the OSI command post. A survey of our vehicle fleet showed that we were short of automobiles. We rented sixteen vehicles for use in the operation. The day before the candidates arrived all OSI agents had been briefed and were prepared. Numbers which could be clearly seen by the US Marine helicopters on patrol over the beach were placed on top of each vehicle. I was directed to take notes for a briefing of our director after the operation. With great effort, OSI agents performed in an outstanding manner. The service OSI provided was invaluable, as was the experience that they gained.

One incident was very interesting. I went to the grounds of the Jackie Gleason Auditorium to determine Governor Ronald Reagan's security needs. I was finally put in contact with a woman who was quite influential in the Republican Party. She was also advising Governor Reagan. She informed me that Governor Reagan had brought with him sufficient members of the California State Police to provide protection for him. He did not need any assistance. The woman and I had a friendly discussion about the convention and she informed me that she did not expect Governor Reagan to receive the nomination this time, but he was planning for another time.

When the convention ended, we went back to Washington to brief the General. He had already been informed by the USAF Chief of Staff of the outstanding job done by OSI. He was going to write a letter to each man who participated in the operation commending him for his performance. Some of the problems we noted made us adjust operating procedures accordingly. The following year we were to participate in another operation related to DVP, only this time we were not providing protection coverage, we were conducting a vulnerability survey to determine how secure the President would be while under the protection of the US military.

The President's Military Assistant was an Air Force Brigadier General. He had been talking to Charlie Sither, who at that time was working in Physical Security at the White House. The General made some comment about how secure the President would be under the care of the US military on the various bases in the Washington Area. Charlie advised the General that if there were any serious vulnerabilities OSI agents could find them. OSI had been active for a long time in conducting vulnerability surveys on USAF bases and quit when they were too successful and the military started looking for OSI agents instead of real enemy agents. Charlie Sither agreed to set up a survey on behalf of the White House. The General advised that if only one of OSI's planned surveys was successful, military protection procedures had to be overhauled drastically.

Charlie Sither was to head the operation, but actual

operations would be supervised by the Chief, Special Activities Branch. I was one of the first called in to be briefed on our new operation. The survey was to involve attempts to gain access to several places where the President frequently appeared on US military bases. Camp David, the President's weekend retreat, was one target, Andrews Air Force Base was a second, the Presidential yacht was another and finally, the US Marine helicopter hanger at Bolling Air Force Base. Attempts were to be made to penetrate these facilities, but there were certain limitations placed on the operation. No penetrations would be attempted on any of those places when the President was present. No force or violence could be used to effect entry to any of the targets. No genuine identification, such as OSI credentials could be used. The agents selected for the operation were broken up into teams. I lead the team that was to target the yacht "Sequoia". There was a team for Camp David and one for the Marine Helicopter Squadron at Anacostia, and another team targeted the President's aircraft at Andrews Air Force Base. All teams were told to start formulating their plan of operations and were to report back in one week with the results.

I was fortunate to have a good team. One member was a Senior Master Sergeant and an agent of great experience. He was also a certified master diver. The second was a young captain who was inexperienced but very innovative and not afraid of details. The fourth member of our team was a Technical Agent, who was also a SCUBA diver. He would prepare the electronic elements of our simulated high explosive device. We spent one afternoon discussing a plan for the operation. Once all agreed on it, we followed it. During the preparation and execution phase we followed the plan and it never changed. We began by using an outboard motorboat that was owned by one of the agents who was involved in the overall operation. Two of us drove past the yacht and surreptitiously took pictures from every angle. The Navy men waved to us as we went by. That evening we went by again to determine the lighting conditions at night.

Once satisfied that we were knowledgeable of the area surrounding the yacht, we went to a small farm in Virginia that was owned by our Senior Master Sergeant's father. There was a creek flowing nearby that was deep enough to practice SCUBA diving and the area was isolated. We acquired two fifty five gallon steel drums that would be our simulated high explosive carrier. The drums, together, could hold about 750 pounds. They would be placed under the yacht, during the early morning hours. An electrical line would go from the device, up the pier, to a hidden place under the pier where a radio receiver could be secreted. The plan was for a radio frequency transmitter, like a miniature radio station, to be used to signal the receiver under the pier and it would detonate the simulated bomb. After some thought, we decided that there should be some observable result after the "bomb" went off. One of the team suggested that dye marker powder be placed where it could be released and float to the surface. This gave off a brilliant green color.

The dye marker was placed in a gallon glass jug and a blasting cap, which had been stolen by our Technical Agent from a local construction site, was placed inside with the dye marker and the jug sealed. The exploding blasting cap would send the dye marker to the surface all around the yacht. We placed the dye marker in the bottle, sealed it and detonated the blasting cap by radio control. The cap exploded obediently, but the dye marker would not cooperate and remained on the bottom of the creek. Our Senior Master Sergeant came to the rescue. He cut up a small log with a chain saw; the resulting sawdust was placed in a bottle and the dye marker mixed in with it. The next time we exploded the bottle, the dye marker powder, which had attached itself to the sawdust, rose to the surface and made a beautiful, bright green circle which seemed to get ever wider as the creek flowed, by the site. We would fasten the jug to the two steel drums, which we had fastened together, and then run the wire from the jug to the receiver under the pier. The receiver was about the size of a walkie-talkie and could easily be hidden under the pier. We continuously monitored the activities around the yacht, almost on a daily basis, to determine if anything would affect the operation. In reconnoitering the area, we discovered that there was a metal dumpster located at the end of the pier at which the yacht was based. This presented the possibility of a "Plan B." The dumpster could be loaded with several hundred pounds of simulated explosives and detonated by radio control when the presidential motorcades approached the pier. Filing that away, we continued with our original plan. There were no difficulties encountered after we worked out the details for our operation. One thing remained, and that was to experience conditions that would be present when we carried out the operation. One evening we went into the water and approached the area where the yacht was moored. Our Senior Master Sergeant went in alone to determine if there were any nets or other impediments that might foil our plans. There were no problems encountered.

On the night of the operation we were able to accomplish our mission without any difficulties. The plan had worked perfectly. At about 08.00 A.M. the next day, I went to the office of the commander of the yacht, accompanied by Charlie Sither, the President's military aide and our Technical Agent. I had blowups of all the photographs that we had taken and used them to brief the commander on what had happened. His face was ghostly white as I described how we had placed about 750 pounds of simulated high explosives under the yacht during the early morning hours. We went over to the yacht, where, with everyone observing, our Technical Agent pushed the button on his transmitter. Almost instantly a "pop" was heard and within seconds a bright green color surrounded the yacht. The President's military aide was speechless and I was dismissed for the day. I went back to OSI Headquarters to find out the results of the other operations.

The operation at Air Force One was a complete success. One of our agents, who was a Lieutenant Colonel, put on Brigadier General's stars and contacted the pilot of the Presidential aircraft and identified himself as a General in the Air Force Reserve from the pilot's home state. He was just ending a two week active duty tour and wanted to see the Presidential aircraft. The pilot was more than happy to oblige him. While being shown through the plane, he placed a simulated explosive device under the pilot's seat. When he was briefed about the operation, the pilot exclaimed, "That's not fair!"

Perhaps, the most original plan was executed against Camp David. First, a team scaled the fence and was able to enter the grounds and approach "Aspen" cabin, which was where the President stayed. It was locked so they aborted the mission in favor of the other part of the team that had been assigned to penetrate Camp David. Two young captains had an OSI secretary listen to the conversation of the secretary in the White House Military Office. They then had her call the commander of Camp David and ask him if the President would be there within the next few days. He said that he would not. She then, posing as the Military Office Secretary said that two administrative aides to Senator Ted Kennedy wanted to spend a couple of days working on a project for Senator Kennedy. The commander said that he would be more than happy to provide a cabin for these gentlemen. The two captains, in a black rental limousine, arrived at Camp David and were personally welcomed by the commander. That evening, they were invited to dinner with the commander and his wife. No one had ever asked for any identification. This was the second time in the operation that the US Navy failed to display any security consciousness, though it would not be the only service to fail.

The fourth operation involved penetrating the US Marine helicopter hanger at the Anacostia Naval Air Facility, which was part of Bolling Air Force Base in Southeast, Washington, DC. The goal was to gain access to the water tanks used for drinking and place simulated LSD in them. Numerous attempts were made to gain access to the hanger. The US Marines, who were on duty there, absolutely refused them access to any part of the facility. When they feigned a good reason to enter, the Marines said that they would be happy to call the Officer of the Day and if he approved their entrance it would be alright. The team realized that this was one place that would not allow any unauthorized entries. They immediately departed when the Marines began to show suspicion.

The operation, as a whole, was almost a complete success. We had achieved our goals in three of the four efforts that we made. There was much embarrassment among those military involved and much was learned about security. While this type of action did not endear us to our fellow military it performed a vital function, that is, to test the on-base security afforded our President.

Our Director was naturally quite pleased with the operation and congratulated everyone involved. I am not aware of any adverse action being taken against any of the military people responsible for the various areas of security that we penetrated. I also never heard about any reaction from the Secret Service. They must have been a little upset to realize that when they turned the security of the President over to the military, there was something lacking, which made their mission all the more difficult. The most significant thing about the whole operation was the fact that, if we were real terrorists, three of the four penetrations could have resulted in death or injury to the President.

Shortly after the White House operation, I was called in to speak with the General about a very sensitive subject – US prisoners of war. The General said that the President would like to rescue some US POWs from North Vietnam. He wanted me and Colonel Russell Wickman to research the possibilities of carrying out a rescue operation. We were to devote all our time to this project. We would have the assistance of the Army and CIA in our effort. We were to begin immediately.

First, we were given a room to work in which was

isolated from the rest of headquarters. We got a map of North Vietnam which was about six by eight feet and placed it on the wall. After coordinating with CIA and Air Force Intelligence, we plotted the location of the POW camp. We also plotted the location of points in North Vietnam which, because of their isolation and lack of population, could be used as a pick up point, if necessary. The CIA allowed us to look at a mock-up of the prison and also sent us any IRs that could be of use to us in planning a raid.

Colonel Wickman and I spent a couple of months on the project during 1969 and completed it at the end of that year. Regretfully, we came to the conclusion that our intelligence was not good enough to ensure that a raid would be successful. The North Vietnamese moved the prisoners periodically and our intelligence lagged by about six to nine months. If a raid took place, there would be no assurance that the prisoners would be in the prison. We also were concerned if there might be reprisals against other prisoners if a raid took place, whether it was successful or not. After checking our research carefully, we went to the General and briefed him on the unlikely success of any raid at this time. We suggested that we improve our intelligence coverage to ensure that a raid at a later time might be successful. After our briefing, the General indicated that he was not happy with the results of our study. He advised that the President wanted to get some prisoners home by Christmas of 1969. That date was fast approaching and there was not enough time left to even properly plan a raid by Christmas. The General thanked us, rather reluctantly it seemed, and we were dismissed.

In June of 1970, the problem was attacked again,

when a USAF Brigadier General formed a task group to undertake the planning and execution of a raid on Son Tay. By mid November of 1970, the raid was carried out. The raiders found that there were no prisoners in the camp. They had been moved in July of that year to another prison. I saw the raid as a symbol of the way the Vietnam War was being fought. There was great bravery, an impatience for immediate results, and a lack of good intelligence to guide planning and operational actions.

Had there been one US resource on the ground, he could have, by simple observation, determined that the prisoners were being moved. He might even have found out where they were being moved. The truth was, we did not have one single resource in North Vietnam who could provide us with the needed intelligence. At this point we had been involved in the war for over ten years. The difficulty with intelligence was the fact that we had no assets that could be successfully infiltrated into North Vietnam. Efforts by the South Vietnamese to place agents in the North were dismal failures. One of the major reasons for the failures was the fact that the North Vietnamese had a very effective CI effort and most agents were caught almost immediately after they entered the country.

I was due for another overseas assignment and was told that I would be eventually assigned as Chief, Counterintelligence Division in the UK. But first, I was to take care of another matter. The North African country of Libya had asked the USAF to close its airbase located near the Libyan capital of Tripoli. OSI had a small District Office there and I was being sent over to close it down.

SHUTTING DOWN IN LIBYA

Libya, a former Italian colony was granted independence in 1951 and was under the rule of King Idris. He was pro-Western and allowed both Great Britain and the United States to have military bases in Libya. As early as 1964, pressure was put on Libya to liquidate the British and US bases in Libya, principally, by Nasser of Egypt. By 1967, both Great Britain and the US agreed to the closing of their bases in 1971, the year in which the agreements expired. Libya had developed its oil resources and was experiencing rapid economic growth. It did not need Western financial assistance and desired that the bases be closed.

On September 1, 1969, a bloodless coup occurred against King Idris. The man who emerged as leader of the country was twenty eight year old Colonel Mu'ammar Qadhafi. He was appointed Prime Minister in January, 1970. From the time of the coup, Libya drastically radicalized its polices, both in domestic and international relations. Libya became a military regime which was completely controlled by Qadhafi. Shortly after the coup, both the US and Great Britain were told to close their bases in Libya.

The USAF maintained an airbase, Wheelus Air Force Base, near the Libyan capital of Tripoli. The base had been used as a training base for bombing practice by USAF pilots from Europe and elsewhere. The island off the coast of Libya named El Watiya, was used for the bombing practice. Because of the outstandingly good weather, planes could fly on practice bombing missions year around. The loss of this base would be a serious one for the USAF and, reluctantly, closing down operations began in early 1970.

Before I left for Libya I had an opportunity to debrief the former OSI District Commander. He was a fluent Arabic linguist and was extremely pro-King Idris. We had excellent relations with the King and this fellow was partly responsible for it. He was a real Arabist and was thoroughly familiar with their culture and customs. Because of his sympathy for the King, he had been transferred from the country shortly after the coup, because it was feared that he was in danger. He was also an accomplished sculptor, a fact that would later cause me grave concern.

I arrived in Tripoli, Libya in February, 1970 and, prior to my departure, had been told that the base would be closed shortly and I would be assigned to the UK. I was met at the airport by an old friend, Special Agent Barry Hennessy.

He and I had been in Italian language school together. I knew him to be a very skilled professional and was pleased to be told that he would be my second in command, at least for a few months. He had been in Libya for over two years and was very knowledgeable about all our CI operations. Unfortunately, he and his wife Sandy, and their newly born son, were looking forward to leaving Libya soon.

The Wing Commander at Wheelus Air Force Base was Colonel "Chappie" James. He was a famous fighter pilot from the Vietnam War and also well-known for his super patriotism. He was highly respected by all who knew him and was an impatient man, who could not tolerate inefficiency or incompetence or anything that blocked mission accomplishment. I was to meet him the next day. The present OSI Commander was temporarily assigned that post when the previous commander had to leave because of his pro-King Idris sympathies. He was happy to see my arrival, since he was to retire as soon as I replaced him. He was a very likeable fellow, who turned things over to me as soon as I arrived.

The next day Barry Hennessy drove me into Tripoli to look around. As we left the base, our car was thoroughly searched. Fifty yards away from the gate, it was stopped again and searched. Just before we reached the limits of Tripoli, we were searched again. Barry explained that this was a form of harassment indulged in by the police to show their disdain for Westerners. I noticed that the black-clad police did not carry a firearm. Barry said that Qadhafi was very careful concerning who was allowed to be armed. The police apparently had not gained the measure of trust needed to permit them to be armed. During the stops, the police were very rude and disdainful of us. This was true for all of them.

Tripoli was a city of two million people and looked like something out of the *Arabian Nights*. It was a busy city and no one seemed to notice us as we drove around unmolested. All the Libyan women observed on the streets were completely covered with a black burnoose, with only one eye showing. The Western women we observed were wives of the American and British oil workers. No one seemed to pay any attention to them either. I would find out later that they really were not comfortable in Tripoli, but had no choice. All their mail and consumer goods had to be received in Tripoli, since they were civilians and could not use military postal channels or the base commissary facilities. Barry admonished me not to feel too sorry for them. They lived in beautiful villas near Tripoli and employed servants to handle all their household tasks. They had their own private school with American teachers, all provided by the oil companies. The "oilers' as the military called them, were very well paid. They often flew to the island nation of Malta, which was free of all the restraints placed on them by Qadhafi. There they enjoyed good food, modern hotels and night clubs. One thing missing from their lives was the availability of alcoholic beverages. Qadhafi strictly enforced the Muslim prohibition against any alcohol. The oilers developed a system of alcohol stills which produced a reasonably deadly alcoholic drink.

One advantage that the military had that was denied the oilers was the fact that we were allowed to maintain liquor and beer supplies in our Officer's and Enlisted Men's clubs. Well aware of this source of alcoholic beverages, the oilers sought to be invited out to the base and frequently invited military people to their homes. It was unspoken, but widely acknowledged that, if you were invited to an oiler's home you would bring a bottle of gin or scotch. Of course you ran a risk of being found out by the police who were sure to search your car as you departed the base. There were more places to hide things than the police could imagine and few people were ever stopped and their liquor confiscated. Barry read my mind and said that the oilers were a poor source of information; they were totally isolated from the Libyan Government, as well as the Libyan general population. What seemed an ideal life did have its drawbacks for the oilers. They were often homesick and most of them missed the US terribly.

Barry Hennessy briefed me on the fact that our CI collection had ended. We knew that if we left the base we would be surveilled by Libyan Intelligence. Any Libyan that we were seen contacting would be immediately hauled in for questioning. There were one or two collection assets who could be contacted because they operated retail stores like rug and furniture dealers. Those people were really running scared and wanted OSI to get them out of the country. That was impossible. It was necessary to reassure them that their relationship with OSI had not been compromised. I knew it was a problem that would not go away.

I made a courtesy call on Colonel James, who was the Wing Commander of a rapidly disappearing wing. Already, people were starting to depart and shut down Air Force facilities. As they left, Libyan soldiers moved in to the buildings they had occupied. Armed Libyan soldiers were already all over the base. We pretended that we didn't notice them; but it was alarming to see them pointing their guns at us as they walked around the base.

Colonel James' sergeant directed me to enter James' office. He was sitting behind his desk and did not rise to greet me. I identified myself as the new OSI Commander. He was very business like and did not ask me to sit down. I told him that I was there to serve him and if he needed anything from OSI he need only ask. He did not react to this promise at all. In fact, he told me that he was leaving soon. He had been promoted to Brigadier General and was being reassigned to the Pentagon. He mentioned some colonel who would be taking his place as Wing Commander. At that time, the "wing" was about a few hundred people. I said, "Thank you for seeing me

Colonel." I then quickly left. I didn't know if he was being rude because I was OSI or because he just didn't like my looks. I vowed to conduct all future business with his replacement.

There was a story going around the base, which had been confirmed by reliable sources, that Colonel James had invited the German Ambassador to his home for dinner. His home was located close to the main gate. The gate was manned by both a Libyan soldier and a USAF sergeant. The Libyan had stopped the ambassador and was about to search his limousine. James observed this and ran to the gate, grabbed the Libyan and tossed him to the ground. At first the Libyan started to make a gesture toward his holstered pistol. He thought better of it and just glared at James. A Libyan officer was visiting the gate and told the sergeant that it was lucky that the Libyan soldier didn't draw his gun because James would be dead. The sergeant already had his pistol out and told the Libyan that if the soldier had drawn his weapon both he and the officer would be dead. James took one look at the Libyan officer and the officer departed.

Another incident occurred which gave me more insight into the famous Colonel "Chappie" James. The base theater was showing *Gone With the Wind*. There was a scene in which Scarlet O'Hara slapped her black maid. At that exact point several black airmen jumped up, exited the theater and left the doors open. This was immediately reported to Colonel James. The next day he had everyone report to the base theater, both officers and airmen. Everyone was sitting there in silence wondering what was going to happen. Suddenly, the entrance doors in the back of the theater burst open, as if they had been dynamited. Colonel James strode down the aisle and ascended the stage. He was carrying a walkie-talkie. He began by referring to the fact that yesterday a racial incident occurred. He looked at the audience with a facial expression of complete anger. He then said, "We are all in a difficult position here. We don't really know what these people may do to us. As United States airmen we are expected to act like men, not racist school boys. If there is even the slightest indication of a racial incident, between a black and white airman, I will court-martial both of them and then kick their butts so hard that they will not need an airplane to get home." He then slammed his walkie-talkie down so hard on the podium that it shattered into fifty pieces. He walked out of the theater, leaving everyone speechless. That was the last time I saw Colonel James; he left for the US the next morning.

Shortly after I assumed command of the dwindling OSI District Office, I received a visit from a young civilian who told me that he was a CIA administrative officer and was the only CIA person left. They had a facility on Wheelus airbase which they gradually closed down. When I arrived, it was almost completely closed. They had asked me to send some packages to the US through Air Force postal channels for them and I did not question them about the contents and agreed to do it. They would bring the packages to my office and one of my sergeants would see that they were mailed through USAF postal channels. This was not unusual because they could not send any mail through Libyan mail channels because they knew that they would be monitored. I thought that assisting them in this way might ensure cooperation from them.

There was a CIA operative on the base who was posing as an Air Force officer. I did not know his mission, nor did I care. He called me over to his office and handed me a document. According to the document, a Libyan national, who had supposedly provided information to OSI, was in fear of being arrested by Libyan Intelligence. He gave the names of several OSI agents he had met with and provided information. One of the names was Barry Hennessy. I looked at the date of the document and it was dated two weeks earlier. I asked him when he got the document and he advised that he had gotten it on the date of the document.

I exploded. I asked him if he knew that anytime during the last two weeks, the Libyans could come on base and arrest my agents for espionage. I pointedly asked him why he had sat on this information. He did not reply. I told him to tell his buddies that the postal service was ended. There would be no more packages sent out by OSI. I would not risk having my people arrested because they had been stooges for the Agency. I alerted Barry Hennessy and the other agents that they would be leaving for Germany on the next flight out. I would write the orders to get them on the manifest. They did leave two days later and I breathed a sigh of relief. My feelings toward the CIA were not friendly. They had endangered OSI people, either intentionally or as a result of incompetence. In either case I wanted nothing to do with them The Libyans had two weeks to arrest my people because of the CIA's failure to notify us of the threat of exposure.

When another young CIA individual, whom I knew slightly, appeared at my office, I was not in a very receptive mood. It turned out that he had been left alone to close down the operation. He was not an Operations Officer and was only knowledgeable about administrative matters. I told him that I would help him as much as I could.

He was given few instructions and he and his wife and two little girls had been living in two rooms of the BOQ. His problem was that he had been given a briefcase that was almost the size of a suitcase. He had been told to "get rid of it."

We examined the briefcase and determined that it was one of the security briefcases used by the CIA and the State Department. If opened the wrong way, it could suddenly burst into flame, destroy the contents and seriously injure the person who opened it. He did not know what to do with it. Because of the classified nature of the briefcase, he had kept it in a closet in his BOQ room. He feared for the safety of his family if it was to ignite accidentally.

We took the briefcase from him and assured him that we would dispose of it. That night Barry Hennessy and I carried the case gently down to the beach, which was adjacent to the airbase. We had a long cord attached to the briefcase and laid the case behind a large rock on the beach. We got about thirty feet away, behind another rock, and pulled the cord as hard as we could. The briefcase impacted on the rock; and suddenly a sheet of flame about five feet high went into the air. We cautiously approached the scene of the blast and saw that where the briefcase had been there was nothing but charred ground. There was nothing left of the briefcase. Even the closest examination of the scene would not show just what had been there before the instant conflagration.

We left the scene quickly and headed for the Officer's Club. A drink was in order to settle our nerves. I jokingly said to Barry, "I hope there are no more problem surprises." Barry suddenly turned serious and said, "Well, there is King Idris' head." I asked for an explanation and was told that the previous commander was a sculptor. I suddenly remembered knowing that, a fact that I didn't consider important at the time I acquired it. Barry explained that the previous commander had sculptured a plaster head of King Idris. When the coup occurred he hid it so that it would not be discovered by the Libyans. It was almost completed, and clearly depicted the former monarch in all his magnificence. With some trepidation, I asked, "Where is it hidden?" Barry replied that there was a trap door in the OSI Office that opened to a small storage space. The head had been placed there and had been there for the past eight or nine months. It had apparently been forgotten.

I tried to imagine what the Libyans would do if they suddenly decided to search the office and they found this remarkable head of King Idris. The next morning, with the door to the office locked, Barry and I took a sledge-hammer and pulverized the King's head. There was nothing left but a fine powder when we finished. He assured me that he was not aware of any other potential problems. Barry and his family then departed for Germany the next day. He would be sorely missed.

When Barry left, I was the only officer remaining. I had about seven enlisted people, two of them agents. I was surprised to find that both of the remaining agents were Arabic linguists. They had been in Libya a relatively short time and so the benefit of their language skills was not fully realized. One of the agents, in addition to being a linguist, was experienced in CI and had completed a tour in Germany doing CI work. Both agents wanted to stay to the end with me. At that point, I did not know what the end was. I had received no word as to when we would depart Libya. It had to be sometime in 1970, but we did not know when. I had sent the secure phone to Germany and thus was unable to contact OSI Headquarters to enquire about our closing date. I attempted to talk to the American Embassy about the closing date but they ostensibly did not know when we would close down. I then remembered a conversation I had with an embassy official when I first arrived. He explained that he had a way of judging the mood of the Libyans. He would ride his bicycle to work and count the number of times stones were thrown at him. I laughed until I realized that he was serious. I considered his novel evaluation of the Libyan mood somewhat imprecise.

The monotony of having little to do was broken when we received a message, through the base, from Air Force Intelligence. The Air Force had been providing training to the Libyan Air Force in various specialties. Although this was not CI, it was positive intelligence and there were no resources to collect this information but OSI. They wanted to know the overall efficiency level reached by the Libyans as the training was shut down. Apparently, there had been no plans to debrief our people as they ended their training programs, or if there were, the sudden closure cut short their plans.

Several instructors, all of whom were senior Air Force non commissioned officers, were called in to our office and asked a series of questions that we had put together. They were very cooperative and provided detailed information, much of it beyond the scope of our questions. They provided precise evaluations of the degree of efficiency and effectiveness possessed by the Libyan Air Force trainees. The information that they provided could be valuable in any overall evaluation of the Libyan Air Force.

We tape-recorded all of the interviews (our secretarial support had left) and sent the tapes, through the base, to Air Force Intelligence. Some of the evaluations were very revealing. For example, according to one senior non commissioned officer, the Libyans had absolutely no concept of preventive maintenance. They believed that if something broke, it was the will of Allah. It was almost impossible to get them to appreciate many of the things that were absolutely necessary to sustain modern air operations. Their methods of making liquid oxygen were so flawed that the oxygen was believed by the instructors to be dangerously contaminated when they used it under pressure.

Another evaluation was to determine the ability of the Libyans to conduct control tower operations. They were capable in this area, only under perfect weather conditions and when only a few planes were involved. According to the instructor, the only air controllers less qualified than the Libyans were the Egyptians. As each instructor was debriefed, a clear overall picture of the effectiveness of the Libyan Air Force began to emerge.

The results of our debriefings raised our morale tremendously. We felt that we were making a major contribution under difficult circumstances. Although the effort was outside our CI role, it was nevertheless an important contribution to the overall USAF intelligence program. With the departure of the last instructor, our debriefings ended and we realized that we had done all that we could. We were reduced to about five people and all operational capability was ended. The only thing left to do was to destroy any files that we had generated, and lock our office. When everyone had left, I closed the office and moved to the BOQ. The remaining days would be spent either in the BOQ or the building that we had converted into a mess hall/lounge. There was literally a ton of food left from the mess hall and we had steaks every night until we longed for something else. The Libyan Army had occupied all of the base, except for the two buildings that we were using. We were very nervous about them peering in our windows and walking by the buildings. All of them were armed.

There were twenty six Americans remaining on the base when someone from the American Embassy came out to the base and told us to be prepared to depart Libya the next day. The aircraft from Germany arrived early the following day and we were all ready. We boarded it and took off in less than an hour. My departure was a great relief and I looked forward to my tour in the UK. Libya was an experience that I did not ever want to repeat. We were literally unable to operate off the base or even communicate with Libyan nationals. Under those circumstances, CI was impossible.

When we left Libya for Germany, I thought about the last several months, when I was uncertain as to what my future held. Despite the fact that we were not physically abused, I knew that the Libyans were unpredictable and likely to engage in violence at any time. I remembered the "exploding suitcase" and "King Idris' Head;" either one of those things could have resulted in our being imprisoned if the Libyans were aware of them. I recognized the dangers that I had somehow pushed to the back of my mind when I was experiencing them. England would be a restful tour.

We were able to close down the OSI Office without too much difficulty and even collect a little intelligence in our debriefings of US personnel who had been advisors to the Libyans. Since the debriefings were an intelligence function, I wondered why the USAF Intelligence had not made plans for them. If OSI had not conducted the debriefings, a lot of good intelligence on the capabilities of the Libyan Air Force would have been lost. This fact pointed out the weakness in our intelligence system. Someone did not appreciate the value of intelligence that could be gained from working daily with the Libyan Air Force. What resulted from our debriefings, when all the pieces were assembled, was an overall view of the Libyan Air Force.

Not surprising was the overall picture of an air force that possessed modern weapons of a sophisticated nature and personnel totally lacking in the education and training needed to effectively operate them. Even under the most trying circumstances we were able to construct this evaluation which had to be of substantial worth.

WORKING WITH THE BRITISH

When the plane arrived in Germany I felt as if I had just been released from jail. Libya was not a friendly place and I was glad to leave there without being subjected to the Arab practice of taking hostages. I looked forward to beginning my tour as Chief, Counterintelligence, in the UK. I had only been on the ground for about an hour when the people in the air terminal at Wiesbaden Air Force Base told me that a plane was leaving for the UK within the hour. It was the aircraft of the Deputy Commander of the USAF in the UK. I walked over to him and asked if he had room for me. He was very courteous and said that I was welcome to a seat.

As the plane came in low over southern England, I saw the greenest land that I had ever seen. It was beautiful. One of the crew members informed me that we were going to land at RAF Stanmore, an airfield located in the suburbs of London, and we were landing on the Queen's birthday. I was told that there was an Officer's Quarters called the Columbia Club, located on Bayswater Road, one of the main streets of London. I bought some British pounds from one of the crew and immediately took a taxi to the club. I checked in and immediately shed my uniform, which I had worn only to avoid any interest in me that the Libyans might have had were I in civilian clothes.

I started walking until I reached Oxford Street and then continued to walk until I reached Piccadilly Circus. It was a long walk, but a pleasant one. I found a fish restaurant (I was all steaked out) and had one of the best meals that I had enjoyed in the last six months. London had to be one of the most exciting cities in the world, as well as one of the most beautiful. The number of shops and restaurants was overwhelming; and I wanted to see every one of them. I took a taxi back to the Columbia Club at about nine o'clock, and realized how far I had walked. After spending my time going between two buildings for a few weeks, the freedom to walk as far as I wanted was exhilarating. I noticed that every block or so, there was a subway stop, known to the British as the "tube." I would find out later that London is the easiest big city in the world to get around in.

The next day I took a "tube" ride to South Ruislip, where the OSI District Office was located. It was located in a small compound, used as a base by the Americans. I went in to meet Colonel James Larson, who was the commander. I had known him slightly when I was assigned to the OSI Headquarters. He remembered me and welcomed me to the District Office. Colonel Larson was an impressive fellow, who looked to be about eight feet tall. He had the graying hair that all full colonels should have and the friendly smile that was very reassuring to someone who had to work for him. He confirmed that I would be the Chief, Counterintelligence Division, and advised that the district had a very active program. In addition to CI collection activity, there were double agent operations in various stages of development.

Colonel Larson introduced me to Special Agent Art Maurel, who was to be my number two. Art was very skilled in CI, even though he had limited experience. He was a "quick study" and never had to be told anything twice. He had been involved in double agent operations and thought that there was a great potential in the UK for those types of CI efforts. The double agent operation was, and probably still is, a controversial operation. It involves using someone who has been approached by or made contact with the Soviets, as a source of information. The double agent ostensibly works for one side, while actually working for the other side. For example, an airman meets a Soviet who makes social overtures to him. The airman reports the contact and OSI determines whether or not the Soviet is an intelligence officer. Then, if the airman is suited to becoming involved in a double life, he is encouraged, with OSI direction, to cultivate the association with the Soviet and see if he is "pitched" or asked to collect information for the Soviets. Sometimes a pitch is a long time in coming and sometimes the Soviet may make a "cold pitch," that is an offer to pay for information without waiting for any real relationship to develop.

Another way a double agent operation may be started is if an airman has a special attraction, such as being assigned to a "sensitive" job. He is "dangled," that is placed in front of the Soviet with the hope that he is approached. Such a "dangle" must be discrete, since the Soviets were very suspicious of any Americans that they encountered. These types of operations were very demanding because the Soviets were suspicious from the outset and it is important to ensure that the double agent does not end up compromised, or truly working for the Soviets. The material that is usually passed is classified, but not of great importance. The idea is not to give more than you get. The case officer, the OSI agent who handles the double agent, must constantly work to maintain rapport with the double agent, while ensuring that the agent remains attractive to the Soviets. It is a very delicate balancing act that does not leave much room for error. For example, if a double agent is asked to take and develop photographs, he must be the one to perform those tasks. If the pictures and film are examined, there must be no evidence that someone else took the pictures and developed them. He must be able to explain exactly when, where, and how he took the pictures and how he developed them. The double agent had to be taught to detect any countersurveillances. If the Soviets surveille him to see where he goes after meeting with them he must be aware of it and act accordingly. Not everyone can deal with the demands that being a double agent will place on him.

Art Maurel was involved in handling the double agent operations for the District Office and doing an out-standing job. He needed some back-up, and I intended to be it. There were five detachments in the UK OSI District Office. These were units of three to five agents who were stationed throughout the UK at the various Air Force bases. There were no USAF bases in the UK; all the bases, though manned completely by Americans, were titled "RAF Lakenheath" or RAF something else. This word game did not negate the fact that we had many USAF bases in the UK. We also had some that were inactive, but for which, I believe, we continued to pay rent to the British.

The presence of the USAF provided a tremendous number of jobs for English civilians, referred to by Americans as "blokes." They were good and reliable workers even though, as Churchill stated, "We were separated by a common language." In subtle ways, they jealously guarded their sovereignty and we were made aware of whose country it was. This was the CI environment into which I was introduced and had to function.

Our CI collection activity was supported by all the detachments, which generally received information for their reports from the British. However, at the time (1970), there was a tremendous anti-war movement in the UK which tried to subvert the young USAF airmen. Vanessa Redgrave, the British actress, and a well-known American actress, Jane Fonda, tried to propagandize our airmen. USAF Headquarters was concerned and levied collection requirements on OSI to monitor the activities of these people. OSI was able to identify the airmen who had been won over and were actively spreading the "party line" among other airmen.

Some of the airmen, who were particularly active against the USAF were, much to their surprise, quickly given honorable discharges and sent home.

I had been in England only a few months, when the OSI District received a message from OSI Headquarters advising that I was to be sent TDY (Temporary Duty) to Naples, Italy, to plan and supervise a DVP operation for Deputy Secretary of Defense, David Packard. He was going to be there to participate in the celebration of the seventeenth anniversary of NATO (North Atlantic Treaty Organization), the military and political alliance participated in by the US in Europe. The OSI District located in Italy had advised that they had no one who could handle such an operation and requested that an "expert" be sent there to handle the operation.

OSI Headquarters decided that I was just the "expert" to handle the operation and ordered that I be sent there as soon as possible to plan and set it up. I would receive complete cooperation from all OSI Districts in Europe. I was also told that the Italian National Police, the Carabinieri, would provide any support that I needed. I was to contact the Carabinieri when I arrived in Naples and also touch base with the commander of the NATO facility at Naples. Before I had a chance to react, I was on my way to sunny Italy. When I flew into the NATO Naval Headquarters at Naples, OSI agents from the Italy District met me and took me to the BOQ. I learned that Lieutenant Colonel Criusti, of the Carabinieri would contact me the next day.

Lieutenant Colonel Giusti was tall, grey haired, meticulously dressed, and able to speak almost perfect English. We hit it off well from the start. We went for coffee, the Italian's favorite beverage, and discussed the scope of the operation, how we would do it and, most important, how many people would be needed. I raided all the OSI Districts in Europe for agents trained in DVP coverage and also got as many vehicles as they could reasonably let me use. We met with the US Navy officer who was to be our point of contact with the NATO naval facility.

Luckily, we got the complete itinerary of Secretary Packard. Only Colonel Giusti, the Navy Liaison Officer, and I had it. We treated it as classified information, and kept tight control of it. We discovered that his wife would accompany him. I had two female OSI agents (we were just starting to really use women as agents) sent from Germany. They would be detailed to full time coverage of Mrs. Packard. The next problem that appeared was that of communications. We had to have communication with all the details during the coverage. I had fifty walkie-talkies sent from the other OSI Districts and four Technical Agents to maintain them. I was to find out later one of the problems involved in having people use walkie-talkies for the first time.

Five days before the Secretary's arrival, we had 100 OSI agents, over eighty Carabinieri officers, plus about fifty Policia Stradale, the Italian motorcycle police. I must add that all of the Italian police assigned were experts in crowd control.

I realized that when we drove through Naples with the Policia Stradale waving everyone out of the way. A rehearsal disclosed the fact that many of the Italian police, except for the Carabinieri, had never used walkie-talkies to any great extent. There was casual conversation all day, and by midday the radios were too weak to operate. Our Technical Agents had to collect them and recharge all the units. The next day I had one of our Italian speaking agents brief the police on the limitations of the radios. They immediately understood the need for sparse conversation throughout the operation.

The operation began, and was carried out without incident, thanks to the professionalism of all the people involved. Mrs. Packard wanted to visit the Isle of Capri, located in the Bay of Naples. Without any hesitation, the female OSI agents, on their own, contacted the police and got a private boat to transport her there. They then accompanied her throughout the visit. Mrs. Packard was a gracious lady who had a great time with the two young, female agents. This incident proved what I had always believed, that women could make great agents, if given the chance. The training of women agents and then assigning them secretarial duties, as had been done in the past, was an unwise practice. When the operation ended,

Lieutenant Colonel Giusti and I were introduced to Secretary Packard as the people who had protected him during his visit. He was generous in his praise, as was his wife, who said to thank the two young women who had accompanied her to Capri.

When I arrived back in England, I found that Colonel Larson had been transferred to Germany, as a sort of Director for the European area. Art Maurel met me and told me that we would be losing Colonel Larson soon. I was greatly disappointed because the colonel was not only a great guy, but he was a professional manager. His theory of management was to surround oneself with good people and get out of the way. His replacement was unknown to me, but we learned that he had no CI experience. As it turned out he was reluctant to venture any opinions concerning CI activities and so pretty much left us alone.

Our CI reporting was somewhat stressing the numbers, without regard to high quality. That was changed. Our reports decreased, but were rated much more responsive than previous reports. One factor that helped was the activities of the Irish Republican Army (IRA), a group of terrorists that the British feared might steal weapons from US facilities. We worked with the Special Branch from Scotland Yard and showed the British that anyone attempting to steal American weapons would have a difficult time. After showing the British how secure our weapons storage facilities were, they showed a gratitude for our cooperation that resulted in much more information from them.

OSI Headquarters advised us that an airman, who had been working as a double agent against the Soviets was being transferred to the UK and we were to handle him.

I immediately assigned Art Maurel to be his case officer. When he arrived he was stationed outside the London area and arrangements had to be made to contact him periodically. He had been approached by the Soviets during a stateside assignment and had been a double agent for over a year. Art Maurel arranged to contact him and find out what instructions the Soviets had given him concerning future meetings with them. The airman had been performing well, and there appeared to be no problems.

The British are very strict concerning the possession of firearms in the UK. Art reported to me that the airman had brought a pistol into the UK. I told Art, "We need to get that pistol from him immediately." Art smiled and produced the small caliber handgun from his briefcase. He had also warned the airman that if the Soviets knew he had a weapon they would immediately suspect that he was really working for the US. Except for that lapse, the airman appeared to be performing satisfactorily.

Throughout the Cold War, there have been many references to the Soviet's use of violence in connection with intelligence activities. On a few occasions they have used violence; but it was the exception rather than the rule. It was an unwritten rule that we did not use violence against each other. Both sides respected that rule. People who were in the intelligence business, who saw it as a violent profession, had what we called the "spook complex." It was always counterproductive to plan for or use violence, when our mission was the collection of information.

Our operations in the UK were subject to control by the CIA. They could veto any operation that they saw as possibly damaging to the overall intelligence effort.

During the time that I was engaged in CI, I never received any information from the CIA that was in the least way significant. I found their people to be unprofessional and arrogant. Years later, after I had studied the Cold War activities of both the CIA and the Soviets, I realized how ineffective the CIA had been. The recent revelations by former CIA members confirms this belief. Their failure to perform effectively, I think, was due to an arrogance that had no factual basis. Their appreciation of CI was minimal, as demonstrated by the Aldrich Ames case, in which one of their own had been spying on them for years. Another factor which resulted in CI being downgraded by CIA was the presence of James J. Angleton. He had been the Chief of Counterintelligence at the CIA for years, and had been one of those duped by the double agent Kim Philby. He had been close to Philby, and when he found out that Philby had been a Soviet agent, he became paranoid. He saw a spy everywhere and ruined the careers of numerous people. I never saw any evidence that he ever actually caught a spy during the time he headed the CIA's CI.

My view of the CIA is that of someone who dealt with them in the area of CI. I was less familiar with their intelligence operations, and they may have excelled in that area. The CIA people in the UK disparaged double agent operations in both theory and practice. They were totally negative in their attitude toward seeking new double agents. They apparently had never read the book by one of their past Directors, John Foster Dulles. In his book, *The Craft of Intelligence*, he describes double agent operations as the essence of good intelligence practices.

We were told by the British MI6, their secret intelligence service, that they did not want to deal with OSI directly, but only through the CIA. There is little doubt that this limitation originated from the CIA. It was, nevertheless, a limitation placed upon us. I never had the opportunity to meet my British counterpart in MI6. MI5, the British CI organization, was very cooperative with us and we enjoyed good relations with them throughout my tenure in the UK. In retrospect it seems natural that MI5, whose mission was CI, would appreciate our goals and provide assistance, while MI6, like the CIA, did not have much appreciation for CI operations. That may explain why MI6 was riddled with Soviet agents like Philby, McLean, Blunt, and others who operated against their own country for a number of years without detection.

OSI, in the UK, was able to operate without much interference from either the CIA or the British authorities. We never involved British nationals in our investigations without immediately notifying MI5. They never tried to restrict our efforts. Actually, MI5 assisted us in several operations. One instance in which they were particularly helpful was when they assisted us in monitoring a "dead drop." A "dead drop" is a location where messages can be left, without detection, so communication can be effected between a double agent and his case officer. The use of dead drops is standard practice amongst all intelligence services. The idea is to communicate without the two ever actually meeting. Usually, the case officer will place a signal, like a chalk mark on a telephone pole, to let the agent know that there is something for him to pick up. It might be instructions, or money. When the agent sees the chalk mark, he goes to the location and unloads the drop. The same is done for communication with the case officer. They do not use the same dead drop, but a separate one, or maybe several alternative ones. Similar in function, is the "accommodation address." It is an address or post box which can be used to exchange communications. The accommodation address can be less secure because it involves the postal authorities. It can be useful to communicate between countries.

I mentioned earlier the importance of surveillance and countersurveillance. Often a case officer is countersurveilled to ensure that he is not followed to his meeting with the agent. The double agent can be surveilled on a sporadic basis to determine what his movements are. He can be questioned later to see if he responds truthfully when asked about his activities. Also, a surveillance may help determine whether or not an agent used countersurveillance techniques. Someone suspected of being an agent will compromise himself if he displays a knowledge of "tradecraft," when he is not supposed to be intelligence trained. The term "tradecraft" describes those practices and procedures used by an intelligence agent to carry out his mission with the utmost secrecy, and the activities of an intelligence organization to reach the same goals. Tradecraft is both an individual and an organizational practice.

A practice sometimes used is the "safe house." This is a place where the case officer and his agent can meet for longer periods of time, if the agent is to be briefed or perhaps placed on the lie detector. The problem with a safe house is that often it is not safe. Unless it is maintained to appear as a normal residence, it may attract attention, particularly from the police. If too many people are seen going in and out, or if it is left unoccupied for long periods, the safe house will attract attention from neighbors and the authorities.

The techniques described make up the tradecraft that must be followed by any case officer who is dealing with an agent. In a large city like London or Washington, DC, there is ample opportunity to practice good tradecraft. But, what of a small town, where all the residents know each other, where there are limited places that offer security for contacts and which require perhaps extensive travel from the large cities? These must be given special consideration and where possible, they should be avoided as places for operations. The large cities are preferred, because of the freedom of movement without observation, the quantity and quality of meeting places or drop sites and the ease with which overall operations can be conducted.

Shortly after I arrived in the UK, one of our agents took me on a tour of "dead drops" which had been used by the Soviets. There were about five sites, spread throughout suburban London. I was upset to discover how professionally selected these sites were. They were located in places where the person servicing the site could see if anyone was watching him and the site could be loaded and unloaded without anyone observing. I found out later that the Soviets employed people who just looked around and located drop sites. While that resulted in the selection of ideal sites, we preferred the case officer to locate their own sites. Particularly in a city the size of London, locating a drop that you did not select might be a difficult task. The case officer must know exactly where the site is, based on his personal knowledge, rather than instructions from someone else. Despite the professionalism displayed by the Soviets in selecting their dead drops, British MI5 was able to set up a remotely operated camera that got excellent photographs of a Soviet case officer unloading a dead drop. The placement of the camera was innovative and was the type of professional effort that got results.

Photography is a valuable tool in CI. It can identify people who an agent meets and places where the meetings take place. It has one limitation; if the subject knows that he is being photographed, the whole operation can be compromised. Therefore, it is usually necessary to use lenses that allow the photographer to be a good distance from his subject. For photographing someone across the distance of a city street, a 300 mm lens is optimal. The lens must be of telephoto length to get an identifiable photo. These were used by us to photograph anti-war protesters.

Photographing a dwelling or other building is useful for a record photograph, which can be examined at one's leisure, thus making it unnecessary to constantly go to the place of interest. Low level aerial photographs can be used to show all the approaches to a building as well as all entrances. If done discretely, photography can be a valuable tool.

Although the British valued personal privacy, they were actively using all the tools that would afford them access to the information that they sought. They appreciated, to a great extent, the fact that certain tools could make up for a lack of manpower. That was important to them, since they were a small organization. One example of their innovativeness was when they used a parabolic microphone (like the microphones used at sporting events) which picked up conversations from about fifty yards away. MI5 used a technique that was extremely effective. Instead of trying to round up people for surveillance work, they had people called "watchers" whose only job was surveillance. They did it all the time and thus they were very good at it.

The use of surreptitious searches, is a seldom used, but very effective CI tool. Such a technique has a great amount of risk associated with it. If the subject of the search is an agent, he will be alert to the use of such a technique and set up "search traps" which will reveal that his place has been searched. A search trap is a technique used to detect a search. For example, the subject could sprinkle face powder on the rug, or the floor, at the entrance to a house or apartment. Shining an ultra-violet light on the floor will show where the pattern of the face powder is disturbed. Ordinary face powder will fluoresce under ultra-violet light. The place where a person walked will disturb the powder and show the lack of fluorescence.

Another practice to thwart surreptitious searches is to measure the distance between objects relative to each other. For example, a desk drawer could be opened slightly by a half inch. If that distance is found to be different, the drawer has been opened. Experienced agents try to overcome such traps. They often photograph the room and the placement of objects to ensure that everything remains in its place. Using a Polaroid camera to photograph the inside of a desk drawer, which has been carefully opened, can be an excellent technique. A surreptitious search team should always carry a camera that can be used to photograph any documents found. Surgical gloves should be worn by all members of the search team, in order not to leave any fingerprints.

The object of a surreptitious search is often to confirm or disprove that the subject is an agent. The presence of classified documents, microdot equipment, one-time pads, subminiature cameras, and other such things, can indicate that the subject of the search is involved in clandestine activity. Classified documents are never permitted to be removed from their storage facility, by anyone. Microdot equipment is photographic equipment that can be used to reduce a page to the size of a period, which can be placed on an innocent document for transmittal. The use of one-time pads confirms that the person is engaged in clandestine activity. The pad is a code device. Each individual using this device has a pad to encode and one to decode. No one can break the code without having possession of the appropriate pad. The rapid development of technology today has added to the picture such items as closed-circuit TV. A room, or even a complete apartment, can be monitored by a TV camera which is slightly bigger than an ice cube. The pictures can be taped or sent to another location nearby. This represents a formidable obstacle for the CI agent hoping to make a surreptitious entry. Such items as "burst transmitters" can send messages in seconds, thus reducing the chance of detection. The ubiquitous cell phone is also a great aid to clandestine communication, though vulnerable to detection.

The tools and techniques just described are all a part of intelligence and CI tradecraft. The CI agent is looking for evidence of a person's clandestine activity. Once that is confirmed, an investigation is carried out to determine contacts and activities. All techniques used carry with them a risk of compromise and must be discretely carried out. If the investigation is carried out with a view to prosecution, then all the legalities required must be observed. Our activities in the UK only involved Americans. We had no authority to investigate British nationals, and we didn't. If the investigation disclosed the presence or participation of a British national then we notified MI5 immediately.

OSI operated against Soviet and Soviet Bloc nationals who were seeking to develop US airmen into spies for their intelligence services. The two principal Soviet Agencies that we were targeted against were the Soviet Military Intelligence (GRU) and the KGB, the latter being more or less equivalent to our CIA. Both organizations operated out of the Soviet Embassy. They usually had "diplomatic cover," that is, they had diplomatic status that gave them diplomatic immunity. The most serious action that could be taken against them was expulsion. All countries use expulsion as a means of dealing with intelligence agents that are caught violating the host nation's sovereignty. In 1972, Great Britain expelled over ten Soviet diplomats. At that time, we had an interest in one and it took us a couple of weeks to find out if our fellow had been among those expelled.

It is always easy for a host nation to expel foreign intelligence officers. It was an effective technique to wait until the intelligence types really were established, and then expel them. Expulsion was usually carried out almost immediately so the intelligence officer had no time to brief his sources or complete activities that he had planned. Our people have similarly been expelled, sometimes for activities and sometimes just as retribution for an expulsion that we might have carried out.

From time to time, American airmen would encounter Soviet intelligence officers, and report the contact, as they were required to do. Many of these airmen were not suited to being used as a double agent. One colonel, who was a fighter pilot, met a Soviet fighter pilot who was assigned to the Soviet Embassy, and was eager to become involved in a double agent operation. The colonel was bright, quick-thinking and aggressive. He was an individualist who did not always respond to instructions. While his individualist qualities made him a good fighter pilot, something which he was familiar with; they did not stand him in good stead in CI. His tendency was to always interpret specific instructions as general guidelines. We needed someone who could think, but also follow orders, when necessary. This colonel would be too difficult to handle. We did not use him and instructed him to avoid any future contact with the Soviet.

While there is no perfect candidate for a double agent operation, there are people who seem to possess the necessary qualifications. The candidate must be involved in or have access to classified information. He (or she) must be intelligent and a team player. There is no demand for the "James Bond" type of individual. The contest will be brains against brains and, usually, not involve any violence. A mid-level non-commissioned officer can possess these qualities. The potential double agent must be an actor able to feign those qualities that the Soviets would find desirable. For example, someone who clearly likes the good life, and has expensive tastes and hobbies would be appealing to the Soviets.

Since most people who work for the Soviets are motivated by greed and a desire for wealth, the candidate must appear to possess those qualities. Recent examples of such motivations are Robert Hansson, the FBI agent who turned traitor and Aldrich Ames, the CIA traitor. Both men received large amounts of money for their treasonous activities. Interestingly, they were both assigned to CI duties in their respective organizations, and both men pursued their careers as spies, undetected, for many years.

Many spies betray their espionage activities through an ostentatious display of wealth beyond what they should possess. Aldrich Ames clearly lived beyond his means. A few financial checks would have revealed his extra income from the Soviets. He attributed his wealth to his wife's assets. Hansson never displayed any wealth, but displayed an interest in intelligence operations that did not involve him. This latter factor, an interest in operations in which one is not involved, was displayed by the American Jonathan J. Pollard, the Naval Intelligence analyst, who spied for Israel. Both Pollard and Ames would have been detected if their organizations had any CI Program.

All of these factors must be considered by the CI agent in assessing whether or not a person might be involved in espionage. Certainly, the display of unaccounted for wealth and displaying an interest in intelligence which is not a part of one's job, are very good indicators of possible espionage activity. All three, Pollard, Hansson, and Ames would have been tripped up, if these two factors had been applied to their activities. Coupled with other indicators, these factors are useful in determining whether or not a person is possibly spying. They can all be ascertained without the knowledge of the suspect. There is an ancient acronym which explains the reasons for a person committing espionage on behalf of a foreign government; it is "MICE." It covers all the kinds of motivation that may induce such activities. M is for Money, I is for Ideology, C is for Coercion, and E is for Ego.

Among Americans, money has often been the primary motivation. Even Pollard, who professed his love for

Israel, received cash, gifts, and vacation travel from the Israelis. Ideology appears to be the least important motivation today. Ego can be a strong motivator; and is probably a motivator, to some extent, in all cases of people getting involved in espionage activity. Coercion used to be a strong motivation back in the 1940s and 1950s. The Soviets used to use coercion in dealing with people who were homosexual and afraid of having their friends and families find out about their sexual orientation. With the acceptance or at least toleration of homosexuality in many parts of society, little opportunity for coercion of homosexuals exists. Motivation can be a key factor in identifying an espionage agent.

The Americans and the Soviets both make use of the motivational factors represented by MICE. The best motivator, if it is sincere and strong enough, is ideology. It fosters dedication and devotion to a cause. Probably, the least reliable motivator is that of coercion. It fosters a resentment which will cause one to seek relief from the threats and blackmail used by the intelligence service. Coercion is frequently in the background, when the intelligence service gets a person's signature on a receipt for money given for services rendered. This makes one pause before revealing the intelligence agency's activities. All intelligence agencies try to get a signed receipt from their agents.

Agents may receive a salary or reimbursement for expenses, or both. They are generally not allowed to keep any money received from the opposing intelligence agency. This is so that a loyalty for the opposition will not be fostered by the money given.

With all of the factors being considered, OSI in England, began an operation involving an airman reassigned from a stateside base. Bringing a weapon with him was poor judgment, but that was remedied and the weapon taken from him. Except for that lapse, he was a good agent who followed instructions and acted the part of someone who was financially motivated. He was given instructions before he left the United States on how he was to contact his Soviet case officer in England. All instructions were given on 35 mm film, which he had to develop. The container for the film had to be opened in complete darkness, or else the film would be instantly exposed and worthless. He advised us of that and we had him open it and develop the film.

Once he had developed the film, he would provide OSI with a print of each frame, and the film would be inspected, but not touched, by his case officer. He was given a good 35 mm camera by OSI that was to be used in his work for the Soviets; he was given instructions in its use and a general briefing on the various types of film that could be used. His knowledge was to be somewhat superficial because OSI did not want the Soviets to wonder about his expertise in photography. He was required to practice photocopying documents until he became quite proficient. All of the skills OSI gave him would appear to be skills he could acquire on his own. By the time his first meet with his new case officer arrived, OSI was satisfied that he would be ready. He was surveilled from his home to the general area of the meeting site. OSI did not inform him that he would be under surveillance. He was picked up as he emerged from the meet site and surveilled to his home. He never failed to return directly to his home after a meet. He lived off-base in a small English village, near his base, with his wife and family.

He had been told not to tell his wife about his activities for OSI and insisted that he had not done so. Since we had no control over his wife and had not vetted her as we did him, we were nervous about her having any knowledge of the operation. He was to be polygraphed shortly after his arrival in England and that question was to be addressed. Historically, he had been a good subject for a lie detector and OSI felt that if he had shared his activities with his wife, it would come out. Later, when he was examined, he came out clean. There was no indication that he had ever discussed his double life with his wife, or anyone else. We did not rely only on the polygraph and he was interviewed at length by his case officer. OSI was satisfied that we had a good, reliable asset working against the Soviets.

Another important question was whether or not the Soviets knew he was acting as a double agent. This question was harder to answer than any other. OSI had controlled his access to classified documents, but provided him with documents that would be of interest to the Soviets. He was presented to them as an asset presently with limited access, but one who would have potential to be of great service, eventually. Whenever our double agent was actively on the move, it took most of the personnel from our District to surveille him and to monitor activity. The operation worked well and we felt that the Soviets were not aware of the fact that our man was a double agent, ostensibly working for them, but loyal to the United States.

There was a universal problem presented by double agent operations. Because of the sensitive nature of the information gained from them, there was a very great reluctance to disseminate the information; in fact, its distribution was extremely limited.

It was so limited that it was questionable whether or not the information justified the effort that went into acquiring it. Information so closely controlled was of limited value.

It was a constant criticism by CI analysts, who were providing the results of OSI CI collection efforts to USAF consumers. According to them, they could never disseminate anything that emanated from a double agent operation. The people who ran these operations steadfastly refused to release the information that they received, to CI analysts. There was never any information provided from double agent operations; even information that would be used for background, for fear that somehow the analysts would release information which could be used to identify the double agent. Double agent operations were extremely time consuming and costly in money and other resources. If the information was not to be used immediately it was worthless. Despite this, the people who ran these operations, the counterespionage people, continued to limit their distribution to practically zero.

It seemed extremely unlikely that those agents who were working as analysts were any less security conscious than their counterespionage colleagues. It also seemed likely that if our people were wise enough to obtain the information, they could figure out a way to disguise its source so as not to compromise their double agents: During my tenure in OSI CI, I never heard of any CI information, gained from a double agent operation, or anywhere else, being compromised by reports released by OSI CI analysts.

I have had conversations with CIA people in which they disparaged double agent operations as being time consuming and relatively unproductive. I think that they had that attitude because they were not successful in developing any double agent operations. This is not a criticism of the CIA. The Air Force had thousands of airmen, in uniform, that would be attractive targets for Soviet Intelligence. The CIA does not have a vast number of clearly identifiable people who would be appealing targets. Perhaps if the CIA and the military cooperated with each other they could share both personnel and expertise. This rarely happens and the situation is not likely to improve because each wants to maintain their "turf", that is, their ability to control operations and decide where the information will go.

One interesting aspect of developing double agents is the room for innovation. For example, a technique has been successfully used by the Israelis and is adaptable to many situations. A foreign person is approached by a case officer who speaks his language and to all outward appearances, is a native of the same country. The foreigner is asked to assist his native country in collecting information which is of great importance. He is told that he owes it to his native country to provide it with information; he is in a position to provide valuable information. He provides it to whom he believes is an agent of his country. This is known as a "False Flag Recruitment." It can only be done when the case officer convincingly appears to be a citizen of the home country of the person sought to be developed.

All of the techniques mentioned are used in intelligence and CI operations. The professionalism lies in knowing what techniques or tradecraft to use in various situations. One of the most masterful CI operations ever used was called "The Trust." This operation, which was carried out by the Soviets shortly after they assumed power, was very successful in identifying and neutralizing Soviet émigrés who were actively working to overthrow the Soviet Union under communism. The operation involved catching and "turning" a few dissidents and using them to neutralize others. By "turning" we mean to take an opponent and through force or other means, getting him to work for you.

The "turned" individual, now an agent, contacts the dissidents outside the country and tells them of a significant opposition group which is active, and working with impunity in the host country. The agent then convinces some of the dissidents that they can enter the country safely and engage in anti-government activities. Perhaps they are allowed to go in and out of the country without interception several times. After they have done that, they might induce other dissidents to enter the country. After a time, all the dissidents are arrested and their operations completely neutralized. This operation stands out as a major CI success and is studied closely today by the CI community.

During the Cold War, when the Soviet Union was actively working against the United States, it was very difficult to conduct intelligence or CI operations in that country. It was a police state which closely watched its citizens and any contact with Westerners was immediately detected. The Soviet Union, like any other major world power, had embassies, consulates, and trade commissions throughout the world. The restraints imposed in the Soviet Union were missing in many of those countries. Many of them were sympathetic to the West. Conditions were greatly improved for conducting operations against the Soviets within the confines of those countries. Sometimes, the US could count on the active support and participation of the various host countries' police and security organizations. In some less developed countries, the host nation was apathetic concerning the Cold War activities of the US and the Soviet Union.

Numerous defections by Soviets, took place in countries outside the Iron Curtain. Sometimes a "defection in-place" occurred. That was when a Soviet changed his allegiance but remained at his job and provided information to the West. Because of the restrictions previously mentioned, when that person returned to the Soviet Union, contact with him was risky and difficult. Then arrangements would be made, if possible, to meet the agent in a third country and periodically debrief him there. Such operations were termed "Third Country Operations." The operation may or may not be carried out with the consent and cooperation of the third country. Obviously, support from the third country is desirable, for many reasons.

Cooperation from the third country made an operation less complicated and lessened the possibility of compromise. If a Third Country Operation lacked the consent of the third country then its complexity and the possibility of compromise were greatly increased. Great care had to be exercised when selecting a third country. Countries like France, which were heavily penetrated by the Soviets, and the UK which lacked security awareness, had to be closely scrutinized before initiating any operations with their knowledge. During the Cold War, Soviet penetration was pervasive and even extended to their recruitment, at one point, of the head of West German Counterintelligence. Many important operations were compromised and agents lost when the US relied on Kim Philby, a Soviet agent, who was under consideration for the job of the Chief, British Secret Intelligence Service, MI6.

The dangers of reliance on another country's support can lead to disaster, and knowledge of this may have prompted a CIA acquaintance to say, "There are no friendly foreign intelligence agencies." Sometimes, an operation cannot proceed without the approval of the host intelligence and security agencies. Those cases must be individually evaluated and the merits and risks of such operations weighed.

In the UK, our choice was made for us. The UK was our ally and had been for years. Though their idea of security and ours did not coincide, they were cooperative, to an extent, and would allow us, in a limited way, to pursue double agent operations in the UK. We were obliged to keep them advised as to the developments in those operations and provide them with a detailed knowledge of the way the operation was proceeding. I did not feel that this framework for operations was a desirable one, but higher authority than I decreed that we would operate in that manner. Knowing the weakness of British security, I wondered if we had not informed the Soviets when we made disclosures to the British.

One type of CI operation that OSI conducts is the "Espionage Investigation." Unlike criminal investigations which may last, at the most a few weeks, the espionage investigation can last for years. It is probably the most demanding type of investigation that OSI conducts. Unlike the "Double Agent Operation," where the individual works with OSI, in the espionage investigation, the individual is suspected of working for a foreign intelligence service against the United States. His conduct must be thoroughly monitored in order to determine if he is in contact with that intelligence service. If such contact has not been established, and the individual is alerted to an investigation, all he has to do is sever any contact with the foreign intelligence service. At that point, any investigation is frustrated and unable to proceed.

An airman, who was under investigation because he was suspected of espionage, was transferred to the UK and we were given early notification of his impending assignment. The designated case officer for the investigation received a voluminous file from headquarters which indicated that the investigation had been under way for a number of months. OSI first determined where he was to work and what his accessibility to classified information would be. Then a reliable airman, who would be working with the suspect, was contacted and given a limited briefing. He was to closely observe the individual during the workday. He understood the sensitivity of the investigation and was briefed on how to contact the OSI case officer under both ordinary and emergency circumstances. Since our suspect was assigned to an up-country base, and not in London, the investigation would be made more difficult. Resources had to be brought to the suspect's location in order to monitor his activities.

The suspect airman was to live on-base and it was necessary to provide some coverage of his activities when he was in his quarters, especially when he might leave at any time and his subsequent activities would be unknown. To ensure that we knew when he was leaving his quarters, we installed closed circuit television in the hallway. The installation would be monitored by OSI

Technical Agents, who were in adjacent quarters. They would be in radio contact with agents outside the quarters who were conducting the surveillance. With that set-up, we would know when he was departing his quarters and the surveillance people would be alerted in sufficient time to follow him.

The airman did nothing suspicious, he in fact proved to be a conscientious worker. The investigation went on for several weeks and was placing a strain on our capability to conduct other investigations. All our criminal investigators were involved in the operation and our technical division was working it around the clock. The case was constantly being reviewed by the case officer and we were getting the results of investigative efforts that had been conducted in the United States prior to his transfer. Since we were a small District Office, it required almost all our personnel to conduct this case. One of the leads from another OSI District in the US arrived and provided information that definitely eliminated the airman from suspicion. He had not been assigned to the place that the suspect had been. We knew that he could not be our suspect. We coordinated with OSI Head-quarters and were tersely told to close the investigation. It had taken hundreds of man hours to bring the case to a successful conclusion and our efforts were only part of the overall effort.

When an investigation is opened, the OSI District in which the suspect is assigned becomes the office of origin and controls the sequence and scope of the investigation. It sends out "leads" or requests for investigative effort, to other OSI Districts and then monitors the completion of those leads. When all leads are completed, assuming no more leads are added, the investigation is then closed by the Office of Origin. If the subject of an investigation is reassigned, the receiving OSI District becomes the Office of Origin and is supported by the accomplishment of leads from other OSI Districts. The District Office monitors all leads and sets forth leads of their own. It ensures that leads are accomplished on a timely basis by keeping track of the progress made by other District Offices. This is very similar to the way the FBI conducts their investigations.

Like the FBI agent, the OSI agent can go to any OSI District Office and find that the same procedures are being followed. This provides uniformity and predictability. Agents can go anywhere in the world, where there is an OSI Office and find the same procedures being used. This does not mean that an investigation is conducted on "autopilot." It is the job of the case officer to determine what leads, or investigative efforts, must be sent out to other OSI Offices. If this is not done completely, and closely monitored, the quality of the investigation will suffer. Here is where the experience and training of the individual OSI agent comes to the fore. To maintain the quality control necessary, OSI supervisors review all work in progress for thoroughness and accuracy. This extensive review is not limited to field operations only. Like the FBI, OSI has a headquarters element for each type of investigation. For example, complete copies of all OSI investigative reports are sent to the headquarters. In an espionage case, the reports would be reviewed by a case supervisor in the Counterespionage Division. He can bring anything of interest to the attention of the highest level of OSI; he can provide advice and assistance to the OSI District down to the working agent level.

While the OSI District in the field makes most of the major decisions in an investigation, its decisions can be reversed or modified by the OSI Headquarters element monitoring the investigation. Rarely has OSI staffed its headquarters with agents who have had little or no field experience. This practice has caused considerable difficulty. An agent with no field experience is hardly in a position to second guess experienced agents who know their job. Fortunately, OSI did not make a practice of making inexperienced agents case supervisors.

While the FBI's authority extends only to cases in the United States, OSI has responsibility for investigation of offenses against the USAF all over the world. The variety and depth of experience that an OSI agent receives greatly exceeds that of the average FBI agent. This is not a generally known fact and OSI does not mind that. The less publicity an investigative organization, particularly in the CI area, receives, the easier it is for the organization to operate unhampered. The FBI is a good example. Over the years it has built up a good reputation; however, the same news sources that aided in this, have now centered their efforts on criticizing the FBI for real or alleged transgressions. The same is true of the CIA. Both organizations have sought favorable publicity, and in the FBI's case, received a large amount of favorable coverage. In earlier days the control of information was easy. Only favorable information was released to the public. Today, in the "Information Age," media coverage extends to every area of government, even those areas that previously enjoyed complete control of information flow. Because of the use of computers, copy machines, cell phones, and various recording techniques, the "leak," as we have seen is easier, more widespread, and usually undetectable.

OSI has received very little publicity; and it works in relative obscurity. Much of what it has accomplished could not have been done had it been the focus of media coverage. Those agencies that have sought media coverage, for whatever reason, have often given more than they have received. Today, when OSI is mentioned, it is usually in the context of its criminal and fraud investigations. We can only hope that it will retain its anonymity.

The media has always touted the First Amendment and America's right to know. What they have never said was that they decide what the public is to know. Most media people are dedicated to just getting a good story, without regard for the national security. A good example was when the press, and other media, released the fact that the US was monitoring Osama Bin Laden's cell phone. He abruptly quit using his cell phone, thereby depriving the US of a good source of intelligence. They not only cut off a good source of intelligence, but revealed that the US had a certain capability. One could argue that Bin Laden would have assumed that the US had the capability to monitor cell phones. The facts do not support this proposition, because until it was publicly announced that he was being monitored, he continued to use his cell phone for most of his communications. OSI has always had a good policy toward the media: It does not talk to them. Period!

All of the operations that I discussed came and went and were replaced by other operations. We were very busy trying to carry out the CI mission. Finally, my tour in the UK was completed and I was accepted as a Professor of Aerospace Studies at Bradley University in Peoria, Illinois. I left OSI in the spring of 1977 and never resumed CI duties again. I have always looked back upon those days when I was working CI as the most interesting and rewarding part of my career. It is an important function that has been too neglected, and this neglect has cost the US dearly. I hope that this story will create an interest in CI, and that interest will create a force to professionalize it and make it more effective.

I was proud of OSI's constant efforts to become more professional. It was advocating "offensive" CI operations, long before that term became a buzzword in the intelligence community. CI work is a demanding vocation that requires persons of the highest intellect. It is, to use that old sobriquet, "A Battle of Wits." I enjoyed taking part in that battle and hope that I made some contribution.

EPILOGUE

Through the years, since I left OSI, I have maintained an interest in intelligence and CI. I developed a library containing the most widely recognized books on those subjects. I have concluded that, on balance, the United States has not done a very good job in CI. As I read how James J. Angleton remained the head of CIA CI for over twenty years by promising not to conduct detailed BIs on Allen Dulles and sixty of his friends (*The Secret History of the CIA*, by Joseph J. Trento Prima Publishing, 2001), I realized that CI was never really practiced by the CIA during the Cold War or after.

When the recent revelations concerning Robert Hansson, the FBI agent who spied for the Soviets for over twenty years, were made public, the FBI had the perfect disclaimer for not detecting him. They emphasized that they had been a criminal investigative organization and were not configured to conduct CI. Those FBI representatives failed to mention that the FBI had been entrusted with the national CI mission in 1948, the year the CIA was set up as the head of intelligence. This feeble excuse appears to have been accepted by Congress and the public.

Today OSI has 1,672 federally credentialed Special Agents. This force consists of 304 officer agents, 721 enlisted agents, and 236 civilian agents. Their mission has been expanded to include protection of our information systems, economic crimes against the Air Force, computer investigations, and in 1997, it set up an

Antiterrorism Specialty Team. This team is prepared to deploy to anywhere in the world to provide counterterrorism CI to USAF units. The DVP operations that were so important years ago, continue to be a special service provided by OSI to USAF leaders and other persons of high rank.

OSI emerges today as an organization that can be proud of its history and confident in the success of its future operations. No longer a stepchild of the FBI, it has established a history of its own of which it can be proud. Its size forces it to shed any excess baggage and concentrate on what is important. The very difficult task of CI continues to be an important part of the OSI mission and I am sure that it accomplishes that mission proudly and professionally.

GLOSSARY

Agent   In AFOSI the principal counterintelligence case officer.

Agent of influence A human collections asset occupying a high position in the target country's government or intelligence service.

Agent-in-place   An agent used to penetrate an intelligence organization, also called a "penetration agent."

ARVN   The Army of the Republic of South Vietnam.

Asset   Someone, usually an "agent," that acts as a clandestine source.

Audio surveillance A procedure used to monitor an intelligence target which involves electronic devices. It may include bugging and phone tapping.

Black operations   Covert operations carried out in such a way as to make them not attributable to the acting organization.

BND   (Bundesnachrichtendienst) Germany's intelligence service, comparable to CIA in organization and duties.

Bona fides   The true identity of an agent.

Bridge agent	Someone who acts as a courier or contact between a case officer and an agent.
Brush contact	A passing contact between a case officer and an agent; something may be passed between them. It is dangerous if either is under surveillance.
Bugging	Placing electronic listening or recording devices in a targeted area.
Burned	When an operative is discovered by the opposition to be working for an agency.
Case officer	An intelligence operative who manages agents. (CIA term).
Centre	The name for the headquarters of Soviet Intelligence.
Chief of station	The CIA officer who manages a CIA station.
Cipher	A code that substitutes letters or numbers or symbols for clear text.
Clandestine operation	An intelligence or counterintelligence activity that is secret.
Clandestine Service	CIA's active arm responsible for intelligence operations; it is called the Directorate of Operations (DO).
Commo plan	The various methods used to secretly contact an agent.
Compromised	When a secret plan or operation becomes

known to the opposition, or to someone who might divulge it.

Concealment device Something that appears to be an innocent object, but actually contains hidden secret materials.

Counterintelligence *(CI)* That aspect of intelligence activity devoted to destroying the ability of enemy foreign agents to collect information. In addition to neutralizing the enemy's agents, it is charged with protecting information against espionage, individuals against subversion and materials against sabotage.

Covert action An intelligence or counterintelligence activity designed to be kept secret.

Cut-out Usually a person who allows a case officer and an agent to exchange materials without fear of compromise. The cut-out receives materials from one and later passes it to the other.

Dead drop A location, known only to the case officer and his agent, where materials can be left in a secure manner so that an exchange can take place without personal contacts. They are frequently left for a short period of time, if not picked up they are recovered to prevent compromise.

Defector Someone, who has access to intelligence and volunteers to work for an opposing intelligence service; he may seek asylum or continue to remain in place.

DIS	Defense Investigative Service.
Double agent	An agent who has been "turned" and who works for the people he was targeted against.
EEI	Pieces of information that provide a structure of needed information. When all EEIs are satisfied, the target is covered, OSI satisfies EEIs by publishing Intelligence Reports.
First Chief Directorate	The foreign intelligence arm of the Russian intelligence service.
Flaps and seals	The use of various proven methods to surreptitiously open sealed letters.
FSB	The counterintelligence arm of Russian intelligence, formerly a Directorate in the KGB (the former name of Russian intelligence).
GRU	Soviet Military Intelligence.
Illegal	An intelligence agent operating in a country without the benefit of diplomatic immunity. Usually infiltrated illegally.
IIViINT	Photographic intelligence often gained from satellite or reconnaissance aircraft.
KGB	The intelligence and security service of the Soviet Union until 1991. It was re-

placed by the SVR and the FSB.

Legend	A cover story designed to protect the intelligence agent from exposure.
Lima sites	Sites which operated guidance systems for US aircraft flying over North Vietnam.
MACV	Military Assistance Command Vietnam.
MI5	British counterintelligence, comparable to the FBI, but lacking arrest power.
MI6	The British secret intelligence service, the British counterpart of the CIA.
Microdot	Photographic reduction of a document to the size of a period. It can be placed at the end of a sentence and be undetected.
Mole	The worst nightmare of an intelligence or security organization, whereby an opposition intelligence service places an agent inside the organization.
Mossad	Israel's foreign intelligence service. Comparable to the CIA.
NVA	North Vietnamese Army.
One Time Pad	Sheets of paper containing five number group ciphers. They can be used to decode or encode messages. One must have corresponding pads to use them.
Provocateur	An agent who incites an organization or individual to act, resulting in the com-

promise or arrest of that individual or group.

Rabbit	Name for individual under surveillance.
Resident	The title of the ranking SVR officer in a Soviet embassy.
Residentura	The name given the Soviet intelligence organization in an embassy, the Soviet counterpart of the CIA station.
Rolled up	The compromise of an operation and the arrest of the agent(s) involved.
Safe house	A house or an apartment which can be used for personal meetings or a center for activities. Because of the static nature of the safe house, it can easily be compromised.
SCIB	Significant Counterintelligence Brief.
Special Branch	The investigative arm of Scotland Yard.
Station	The operating unit of the CIA that is usually operating out of a US Embassy
SVN	South Vietnam.
TACAN	Electronic aid to navigation.
TDY	Temporary duty.
Technical Agents	OSI or CIA agents whose primary duties involve counter surveillance or positive surveillance activities.

Tradecraft	The practices and procedures used by an intelligence organization to carry out its clandestine activities.
USAF	United States Air Force.
VC	Viet Cong.
VNAF	Vietnamese Air Force.
Walk-in	Someone who has indicated either a desire to escape from his native country or a desire to remain in his own country and work for opposition intelligence.

RECOMMENDED READING

Andrew, Christopher, *For the President's Eyes Only*, New York, Harper Collins, 1995.

Andrew, Christopher, and Oleg Gordievsky, *KGB: The Inside Story of Its Foreign Intelligence From Lenin to Gorbachev*, New York, Harper Collins, 1995.

Andrew, Christopher, and Vasily Mitrokhim, *The Sword and The Shield; The Mitrokhim Archive and the Secret History of the KGB*, New York: Basic Books, 1999.

Bamford, James, *The Puzzle Palace*, Boston, Houghton Mifflin, 1984

Gates, Robert, M, *From the Shadows*, New York, Simon & Schuster, 1996.

Laqueur, Walter, *A World of Secrets; The Uses and Limits of Intelligence*, New York, Basic Books, 1985.

Richelson, Jeffrey T, *The US Intelligence Community*, 4`h ed, Boulder, Co, Westview Press, 1999.

Shannon, Elaine and Ann Blackman, *The Spy Next Door, The Extraordinary Life of Robert Philip Hanssen The Most Damaging FBI Agent in US History*, New York, Little Brown & Company, 2001.

Weber, Ralph, E. *Spymasters: Ten CIA Officers in Their Own Words*, Wilmington, DE, SR Books, 1999.

Wise, David, *Nightmover*, New York, Harper Collins, 1995.

Winterbotham, F. W., *The Ultra Secret,* New York, Harper and Row, 1974.

Wright, Peter, with Paul Greenglass, *Spycatcher: The Candid Autobiography of a Senior Intelligence Officer*, New York, Viking, 1987.

Printed in the United States
114160LV00001B/57/A